Wagadu
Volume 7

Today's Global Flâneuse

Wagadu
Volume 7

Today's Global Flâneuse

Kathryn Kramer

To order additional copies of this book, contact:
Xlibris Corporation
1-888-795-4274
www.Xlibris.com
Orders@Xlibris.com
58418

Wagadu Volume 7: Today's Global Flâneuse
Guest Editor: Kathryn Kramer, SUNY Cortland
© 2011 *Wagadu: A Journal of Transnational Women's and Gender Studies*
Center for Gender and Intercultural Studies
State University College at Cortland
PO Box 2000, Cortland, NY, 13045
www.wagadu.org
Mechthild Nagel, SUNY Cortland, Editor-in-Chief
Tiantian Zheng, SUNY Cortland, Managing Editor
Kathryn Coffey, SUNY Cortland, Book Review Editor
Jean Young, Cornell, New Media Review Editor
Justin Stewart, SUNY Cortland, Webmaster

Table of Contents

Preface
Mechthild Nagel... 9

Editorial
Kathryn Kramer 11

Qu'implique flâner au féminin en ce début de vingt et unième siècle? Réflexions d'une ethnographe à l'œuvre sur la place de Catalogne à Barcelone
Nadja Monnet... 21

The Nomadic Experiment of a Steppe Land Flâneuse
Dianne Chisholm 39

Walking the Wall: Global Flâneuse with Local Dilemmas
Kinga Araya 56

Kyoto blog
Lori Ellis 71

Site-seeing
Meggan Gould.. 78

Stroller Flâneur
Katerie Gladdys 82

she's walking . . .
Henry Gwiazda 85

Preface

Mechthild Nagel, Editor-in-Chief of Wagadu: A Journal of Transnational Women's and Gender Studies with Kassim Kone, Assistant Editor, Wagadu

With this volume, *Wagadu: A Journal of Transnational Women's and Gender Studies* launches its fifth paperback edition, after publishing Volume 3 on "Water and Women in Past, Present and Future," Volume 4 "Intersecting Gender and Disability Perspectives in Rethinking Postcolonial Identities," Volume 5 "Anti-Trafficking, Human Rights, and Social Justice," and Volume 6 in conjunction with the *Journal of International Women's Studies* on "Women's Activism for Gender Equity in Africa and the Diaspora." All volumes, including Vol. 1 and 2 on critiques of imperialism and women in a global environment, can also be found free of charge at http://wagadu.org. The journal is housed in the Center for Gender and Intercultural Studies at the State University of New York, College at Cortland, USA. We continue to receive support from a diverse and international advisory and editorial board membership, making *Wagadu* one of the notable postcolonial and feminist journals (online or in print). The next volume, edited by Susan Dewey, is dedicated to the theme on "Demystifying Sex Work and Sex Workers."

Wagadu: What's in a Name?

Wagadu—the Soninke name of the Ghana Empire—controlled the present-day Mali, Mauritania and Senegal and was famous for its prosperity and power from approximately 300-1076. It constituted the bridge between North Africa, the Mediterranean and Middle Eastern worlds and Subsaharan Africa. Ghana gave birth to the two most powerful West African Empires: Mali and Songhay. The modern country of Ghana (former British Gold Coast) derives its name from the Ghana Empire.

Legend says that Ghana's power derived from a mythic python, which generated the rich gold deposits and controlled the fortunes of the empire. Year after year the people of Ghana had to offer the most beautiful virgin to the python as a sacrifice. One year, the distressed fiancé of a sacrificial girl took a sword and beheaded the mythic python in a preemptive move. The head flew and crashed into the parts of West Africa that became gold-producing regions, leading to the rise of the Mali Empire. Ghana fell after seven years of drought and poverty forced the Ghana people, the Soninke, to disperse and adopt exodus as a way of life to this day.

Why Wagadu? Wagadu has come to be the symbol of the sacrifice women continue to make for a better world. Wagadu has become the metaphor for the role of women in the family, community, country, and planet. The excerpt below from a Soninke song best summarizes this fact:

> *Duna taka siro no yagare npale*
> The world does not go without women.

We hope you will find this volume engaging as the contributors present feminine dimensions of flânerie's revival in the 21st century, edited by Kathryn Kramer, Associate Professor of Art History at SUNY Cortland.

Cortland, December 2010

Editorial: Today's Global Flâneuse

Kathryn Kramer

State University of New York at Cortland

Abstract

Flânerie's measure of the urban featuring a bourgeois, indolent male wandering around newly industrializing cities for the sake of art and modernity is definitely an outmoded metric. Contemporary urban discourse now admits flânerie's fruitful application not only to the urban but also to the suburban and peri-urban and well beyond the male-centered, Franco-European roots of the original concept. This special issue explores the multivalent possibilities of the dynamic flâneuse on the 21st-century global stage.

Preamble

To attempt to define *flânerie* is to get lost in a prickly bramble of urban rhythms, decay, planning, demolition, alienation, construction, voyeurism, renewal, melancholy, expansion, celebration, consumption, and spectacular display—an exhilarating brew of sociology and poetics. And if the blatant mixed metaphor of "bramble" and "brew" may offend, it speaks nevertheless to the collision of disparity that characterizes urban experience—country clashes with city, private with public, past with present, slow with fast. Allusions to nature's weedy remnants along city streets and to an intoxicating aesthetic traversal of those streets, respectively, "bramble" and "brew" bracket terms describing rapid urban transformation and its affective intensity, which is flânerie's preferred milieu for the recording and analysis of metropolitan sensations. Of course, my wide-ranging and excessively serial list applies not only to the effort at coming to conceptual terms with flânerie, but also to the practice itself.

Flânerie probably derives from the French verb *flâner*, which means to stroll, to loiter, to dawdle, and at its most literal denotes idling, pedestrian pleasantry. The practitioner of flânerie is a *flâneur/flâneuse*. An excursive, restorative nature walk that induces poetic reverie and even poetry itself may come to mind. Indeed, the creative transcription of pleasure attained from walking through the natural world is almost as old as the hills that inspire it. Flânerie at its most sophisticated does involve leisurely walking that produces creative work, but it certainly does not evoke a distant, georgic past. Nevertheless, it is true that rural inflections often filter through the discourse of flânerie. Consider, for example, the notion of "intra-urban walking tours" to discover the "urban picturesque" with the purpose of tidying a city's chaotic multiplicities (Bramen, 2000) or of identifying a good spot for a bit of urban-design adjustment (Isaacs, 2000). Yet the typical 18th-century picturesque sketching tour that sought to domesticate the wilderness by distilling it into Romantic imagery is much too reductive to encompass the complex products of flânerie's urban engagement. Social philosopher Walter Benjamin, flânerie's preeminent theoretician, is much better at utilizing the trope of rural wandering toward defining its urban version, and his characterization from the essay "Berlin Chronicle," bears quotation at some length:

> Not to find one's way in a city may well be uninteresting and banal. It requires ignorance—nothing more. But to lose oneself in a city—as one loses oneself in a forest—that calls for a quite different schooling. Then, signboard and street names, passers-by, roofs, kiosks, or bars must speak to the wanderer like a cracking twig under his feet in the forest. (1999, p. 598)

Benjamin's references to acute urban immersion induced through wilderness-guide savvy are ubiquitous throughout *The Arcades Project*, his unfinished yet encyclopedic study of 19th-century bourgeois Paris (Benjamin, 2002). In the section of *The Arcades Project* dedicated to the flâneur, known as **Convolute M**, Benjamin exhaustively documents descriptions of forest-scout acumen applied to municipal prowling by the wildly enthusiastic French fan base of James Fennimore Cooper's *The Last of the Mohicans* (1826), everyone from Dumas to Balzac to Hugo and beyond (pp. 416-449). Benjamin declares these novelists to be indebted to Cooper for their ability to give "scope to the experiences of the hunter" in their urban settings (p. 439). A hunter's keen senses serve "the principle of flânerie," which requires an intense, multisensory experience of city inhabitants, venues, scenes, and landmarks in order to properly detect modernity's metropolitan routes and detours so that "a new Romantic conception of landscape emerges—of landscape that seems, rather, to be a cityscape . . . ." (p. 420).

So far, my present discussion of flânerie's rural traces digresses considerably from more conventional introductions of a practice that emerged in conjunction with the industrializing, modernizing cities of 19th-century Europe. In fact, the beginning of flânerie's praxis away from mere urban idling toward the weightier responsibility of taking a city's measure—most notably in Charles Baudelaire's 1863 essay, "The Painter of Modern Life" (Baudelaire & Mayne, 1970)—roughly coincides with the coining of the term *urbanization* in 1867 (De Baan, Declerck, Patteeuw, Sigler, & Frausto, 2007, p. 17).

And while it might seem that the emergence of such a neologism would mark a widening distinction between the rural and the urban, its appearance actually marks the beginning of discourses that recognize the narrowing of the city/country divide. Now, almost 150 years after the coinage of *urbanization* signaled cities' expansion, *rurbanization* and *peri-urbanization* are among the newest maxims to account for the extent of this growth. The more familiar *suburban* and *urban sprawl* are of older vintage and perhaps more prone to characterizing fringy edges between the urban and the rural rather than their out-and-out blurring by 21st-century globalization's border-transgressing flows of information, goods, and people.

Make no mistake: today's mingling of city and country skews urban. There is no returning to the traditional equilibrium (not that it ever truly existed) of longstanding between the country and the city, with "country" standing in for originary purity and "city" for civilization's necessary evils, generally inclining in the western popular imagination toward favoring the pastoral. In *Imagined Country*, urban geographer John Rennie Short accounts for the pastoral's persistence over centuries due in part to initial mistrust of sweeping change brought on by urban development and the market forces that accompany it, mistrust so ingrained that it forged the stuff of pastoral myth (Short, 2005, p. 31). The anti-pastoral, urban myth of the city as the true source of cultural production, which took shape during the Enlightenment, is not available for reprise either: it fell much faster than its pastoral counterpoint in the face of the inevitable cycles of urban decline. Today, city and country are shot through with each other's traits, rural greenery wired with urban circuitry, the concrete jungle submitted to sustainability. Such is the nature of the "third urban revolution" (with urban emergence and urban industrialization comprising the first and second revolutions, respectively) that becomes a global phenomenon whereby an unprecedented, predominantly urban earth witnesses new ecosystems produced by megalopolitan agglomerations. Conversely, post-industrial metropolitan centers may recover their environmental prehistories (Short, 2006, pp. 177-187). The statistically laden Venice Architecture Biennale of 2006, "Cities, People, Society, Architecture" and its subsequent re-presentation at London's Tate Modern as "Global Cities" in 2007 feature a statement by curator Richard Burdett that embodies the notion of the third urban revolution:

> The 21st century will be the first truly urban era, in which more than 75% of the world's population will live in urban areas, much of it in mega-cities with more than 20 million inhabitants concentrated in the countries undergoing rapid development in Asia, Africa and South America. In the meantime, many Western and European cities are shrinking, or have been forced to re-invent themselves in order to adapt to a post-industrial condition. (Burdett, 2006)

The above discussion may seem at the moment like a rather circuitous path through urban environmental history just to make the point that Walter Benjamin's ambulant urban-connoisseur-as-forest-scout metaphor anticipates current thinking about the rural/urban divide. I hope, however, that it soon will become clear that Benjamin's prescience will also apply to the particular positioning of the flâneuse on today's global stage, which is the theme of this special issue of *Wagadu*.

Flânerie Then and Now

A solitary, eccentric yet respectable urbanite with a touch of the dandy and a leisurely gait, the flâneur was a fixture on 19th-century Parisian thoroughfares as soon as they could enhance unhurried perambulation with a certain pedestrian right-of-way, sufficient "crowd cover," and magnetic urban display. Throughout the first of half of the century, the shopping passages known as arcades that appeared throughout metropolitan Europe, with a particular concentration in Paris, quickly became preferred sites for flânerie. Arcades' glass-ceilinged corridors admitted just enough of the natural environment in the form of light and sky to confer a certain landscape status upon their passages, which in their early days often housed further simulations of landscape in the form of dioramas and panoramas (Benjamin, 2002, pp. 527-536). The glittering, mercantile window displays lining the arcades were the "flora" that completed these walkways' "urban naturalism." Obviously, the arcades were not typically rural, picturesque paths yielding the contemplative rewards of ruined abbeys amidst overgrown foliage. Instead, their picturesque pleasures rewarded a consciousness more reflexive, more *kaleidoscopic*, as Baudelaire describes it, a consciousness prone to an instantaneous immersion into the mutable disarrays of merchandise and people (Baudelaire & Mayne, 1970, p. 9). Like *kaleidoscopic, phantasmagoria* describes a pre-cinematographic visual experience; it is a term for a magic lantern performance by which the means of projection are hidden and therefore heighten a "supernatural" effect to viewers not yet accustomed to the moving image. Benjamin invented the notion of "phantasmagoria of the urban" to apply to the dreamlike fantasies that intermingle with one's waking experience of modern cities (Pile, 2005, pp. 19-20). It is not surprising that both Baudelaire and Benjamin would chose such terms of ocular derangement: they characterize flânerie as confronted by urban modernity's dizzying overlap of banal everyday street life with architectural demolition and construction, rekindled memories of what was there before, commodity display, and all the new media comprising the urban spectacle. From the very start, this experience has been astonishing as well as both mobilizing and distracting, and today it is extended and even overwrought by the effects of 21st-century globalization. Right now, the terminological currency for the intertwining of the quotidian and phantasmagoric throughout today's burgeoning megalopoli (especially applied to those beyond the strictly urban as well as beyond the west) is "urban imaginary" (Cinar & Bender, 2007), which despite its contemporaneity increasingly requires old-fashioned flanerie's embodied sensibilities for its artistic and intellectual rendering.

By the second half of the 19th century, both kaleidoscopic and phantasmagoric consciousnesses were well on their way toward creating future urban imaginaries, magnified as they were by the ever more spectacular deployments of urban design, planning, and architecture that burst out of the Parisian arcades and onto the sidewalks and boulevards broadened by Napoleon III's "urban renewal" policies (Harvey, 2003). More fluvial crowds (efficiently thinned-out by omnibus transportation vastly improved by the macadam-smoothed rides) enabled a better drift for the flâneur whom Benjamin promotes from scout to detective (2002, pp. 439-442). Flânerie throughout wider Paris provided the flâneur with greater opportunities to derive pleasures and shocks from his observation of the urban experience, which he would ultimately recode into a poetics informing his literary, visual, and intellectual work. His insistently commodity-resistant and somewhat undercover glide through the crowd served as a critical thinking tool for a simultaneously subjective immersion in and dispassionate representation of the modern metropolis, and for this Benjamin elevates flânerie yet again—now to the level of the scientific—with the memorable description "botanizing on the asphalt" (Benjamin & Demetz, 1986, p. 36).

Benjamin's constant tinkering with the flaneur's "professional profile" throughout **Convolute M** (scout, hunter, detective, botanist, geologist, artist, journalist . . . the list goes on!) reflects a valiant effort to fashion an iconic figure who stands in for something as complex as the metropolitan spaces of economic expansion yet who is not only standing in for, but also passing considerable time amongst, the everyday life of the boulevard, "and thus, as it were, exhibiting it" (2002, pp. 446-447). Baudelaire went through similar machinations, which is well recounted in Mary Gluck's "The Flâneur and the Aesthetic Appropriation of Urban Culture in Mid-19th-century Paris" (Gluck, 2003). Baudelaire must be credited with one of the first truly critical attempts to elevate the flâneur from a marginal, indolent ambler to artist-flâneur who produces creative work from the exploration, observation, and reading of everyday urban life. The critical theorist Susan Buck-Morss, one of Benjamin's keenest interpreters, updates his notion of "industrious, productive flâneurs" (2002, p. 454), as "ur-forms" of modern intellectuals (1991, p. 304). Buck-Morss's insight slightly post-dates "die Wende" of 1989 and slightly precedes a related sea change in scholarly thinking about urbanism as filtered through a variety of disciplines in a globalizing world. This interdisciplinary turn, often characterized as "affective," registers vastly different modes of reacting to and then shaping the topography of emerging and expanding cities; it reinforces the importance of spontaneous and visceral reactions—marked by an emotional range from pleasure to trauma—for the consideration of the urban experience as it is happening. Lauren Berlant refers to a "sensualist turn" that "originates in an embodied subjectivity, at once overdetermined and permeable to contingent events" (Berlant, 2004; Seigworth & Gardiner, 2004). A new profession gets added to Benjamin's list in the course of these "turns"—that of an ethnographer whose experiential fieldwork now takes a "performative turn" (Foster, 1995; Koepping, 2005). Obviously, the bibliography of the theoretical retooling of urban theory and practice dating from the early 1990s is vast, but Katarina Nylund's "Cultural Analyses in Urban Theory of the 1990s" is an excellent summation of this phenomenon (Nylund, 2001) as is

Ash Amin's "Re-thinking the Urban Social" (Amin, 2007). Certainly there is plenty of evidence that (concurrently with the explosion of globalization and world cities) a new incarnation of decidedly transdisciplinary scholars with urbanist inclinations readmit subjective and aesthetic dimensions into their analyses. Rededication to autoethnographic circulations commenced throughout the 1990s and continues to this day. Not surprisingly, affective "aesthetico-sociology" in combination with globalization reinvigorated flânerie as a valuable device for scholars and artists to navigate and represent the sensual bombardment of world cities. The aesthetic walking practice's fruitful application far beyond its original proving ground of 19th-century Paris and its male-centered, Franco-European roots was re-established.

Flânerie's Revival with a Feminine Focus

My original Call for Papers for this special issue of *Wagadu* was intended to elicit contributions that would explore the possibilities of a fully dynamic flâneuse in the world cities of the 21st century. Evidence of the female urban stroller during flânerie's first round is scant since a woman could not maintain the necessary incognito or enjoy the required free passage throughout the typical 19th-century city, although there are exceptions. For example, Karin Baumgartner presents a very convincing case for Helmina von Chézy, a correspondent for the journal *Französische Miscellen*, providing guidelines as early as 1803—almost pre-arcades era—on how to experience urban space as a woman (Baumgartner, 2008). An important body of scholarly work (which the contributors to this special issue review in detail), dating from the feminist priorities of the 1980s, revises notions of the flâneuse's relative visibility in the 19th century. This scholarship asserts the flâneuse as a distinct reality in the 19th-century metropolis of the west, making a convincing case that public (so-called "masculine") and domestic (so-called "feminine") spheres were not so mutually exclusive as to completely preclude a proactive feminine presence in the streets. Just as her male counterpart, the flâneuse could, within certain limitations, achieve some anonymity on the street, be a detached observer, and produce art and social criticism from her experience. In *Streetwalking the Metropolis: Women, the City, and Modernity*, Deborah Parsons offers another, tantalizing scenario regarding the flaneuse's "absence" on 19th-century streets: she is actually hiding in plain sight as the feminine side of the typically dandified and androgynous flâneur, that her incorporation informs his love of masquerade and fine-tuned, emotional receptivity to the city's sensations as well as reflects a growing male anxiety about the liberalization of public life (2000, p. 26).

Urban public life in the west became increasingly available to women by 1900. Just as a feminine filtration of the 20th-century urban would seem to be imminent, however, the significance of flânerie's embodied process declined and with it the importance of its gendered dimensions. Modern western cities' increasingly prescribed routes, commodified pathways, and "heritage walks" managed flânerie to the point of near nonexistence. It has only been within the last two decades that the rapid and radical transformation in world cities from South America to Africa through the Indian subcontinent and Asia has renewed flânerie's credibility as an effective way through the unpredictable and transformative conditions inherent in today's urban spaces, rife with the creative chaos of self-generating networks of technological, economic, cultural, migrational, and even microbial flows. At the turn of the 21st century, flânerie was rekindled as a subjective process involving all five senses recording at full bore, and the examination of this reinvigoration in terms of the flâneuse's urban experience was overdue.

In response to my Call for Papers, I was expecting submissions of complex, experiential, and emotive documentations of the dynamics of today's world cities from the flâneuse's perspective, twining the aesthetic and sociological threads of her experience into visual and/or verbal renditions, providing not only vivid documents of cities in transformation but also representing their urban imaginaries. Indeed, I did receive complex, experiential, and emotive accounts as the reader will discover, but some reflect more of the interurban circuit created by 21st-century globalization rather than the world cities themselves (Chisholm, Araya, Gould). These authors are more global nomad than flâneuse perhaps, practicing a broader, more cosmopolitan form of flânerie than the strictly urban variety. Even more at odds with my original concept were other submissions that posited flânerie for regions neither urban nor rural, which I described earlier in this editorial (Chisholm, Gould, Gladdys, Gwiazda). Perhaps the most faithful to traditional flânerie is Ellis's blog about Kyoto. Still, while decidedly urban, Kyoto doesn't fulfill nearly enough of the criteria for a world city as developed by the Globalization and World Cities Research Network (http://www.lboro.ac.uk/gawc/).

At first, I thought that the nature of these submissions may indicate that flânerie could not yet be confidently or consistently performed by women on a world city stage, and certainly Monnet's autoethnographic experiment in a busy Barcelona plaza may confirm this suspicion in part. It was unavoidable also not to think that 21st-century female flânerie was taking place on peripheries, was still marginalized. However, as I pondered such possibilities, I realized that certain assumptions of my CFP were flawed: I had committed the error informed by what Janet Wolff so aptly terms "a politics of correction" that has generally been motivated by the imperative to challenge and contest an androcentric universe, to correct its one-sided terms and assertions, to fill its gaps and to modify its canon (Wolff, 2000, p. 34). Wolff says this is a laudable but misplaced motivation, and I agree. Today's global flâneuses as represented by the authors/artists in this special issue are not on the margins of world city flânerie, but rather at its frontiers as globalization redefines the sites that may newly accommodate their walking practices.

And it is just those aesthetic walking practices featured by each of the present contributors that link them to traditional flânerie more than their venues. No theorist of flânerie past or present, even when they come up with witticisms such as "driveur" or "phoneur," denies that being afoot is the only real way for bodies to absorb sensory stimuli necessary to gauge urban vitality. In "What We Talk about when We Talk about 'Walking in the City'," Brian Morris states " . . . even the most automobile-oriented and/or technologically mediated contemporary urban environments still exist as sites of meaning and desire articulated through walking practices" (2004, p. 693). A new buzzword, "walkability," not only confirms Morris's claim, but also often serves to identify those emerging extraurban sites that increasingly invite flânerie (Ewing, Handy, Brownson, Clemente, & Winston, 2006; Forsyth & Crewe, 2009). So, walking remains central: the best way to interact with urban space is still to hit the pavement. The problem these days is defining "urban space."

The present volume's contributors are immersed in labyrinths of the urban, interurban, extraurban, nomadic, and diasporic. Their pedestrian experiences would shatter Baudelaire's kaleidoscope, yet they maintain strong ties to classic flânerie in that they translate their wanderings into a combination of art and social science. As a mode of analysis combining aesthetic, geographic and ethnographic attention to the urban experience, Baudelaire's and Benjamin's flânerie was relational aesthetics *avant la lettre*, an insight clearly foregrounded by the pieces in this issue. The elision between the aesthetic and the sociological is almost seamless in the works included here, all of which partake of the visual, subjective, memoirist, and sociological in measured doses.

Today's Global Flâneuse is a departure for *Wagadu* in that it is a hybrid of sociology and aesthetics. I would like to take this opportunity to thank Mechthild Nagel, *Wagadu* Editor-in-Chief, for agreeing to experiment with the journal's standard conventions. Most of all, I am very grateful to the efforts of Justin Stewart, Assistant Web Developer (although his work for this issue amounted to a job description of Copy Editor and Art Editor rolled into one) whose expertise made it possible to realize the inclusion of time-based media in the HTML version of this issue. The importance of capturing the intrinsic mobility of flânerie with appropriate media cannot be overstated, and this mobility requires appropriate reproduction as well. I would also like to thank Kathryn Russell, Andrew Fitz-Gibbon, and Daniel Harms for strategic support at crucial moments.

References

Amin, A. (2007). Re-thinking the urban social. *City*, 11(1), 100-114.

Baudelaire, C., & Mayne, J. (1970). *The painter of modern life and other essays*. London, UK: Phaidon.

Baumgartner, K. (2008). Constructing Paris: Flânerie, female spectatorship, and the discourses of fashion in *Französische Miscellen* (1803). *Monatshefte*, 100(3), 351-368.

Benjamin, W. (2002). *The arcades project*. Cambridge, MA: Harvard University Press.

Benjamin, W., & Demetz, P. (1986). *Reflections: Essays, aphorisms, autobiographical writings*. New York, NY: Schocken Books.

Benjamin, W., Jennings, M. W., Eiland, H., & Smith, G. (1999). *Walter Benjamin: Selected writings. vol. 2, 1927-1934.* Cambridge, MA: Belknap Press of Harvard University Press.

Berlant, L. (2004). Critical inquiry, affirmative culture. *Critical Inquiry,* 30(2), 445-451.

Bramen, C. T. (2000). The urban picturesque and the spectacle of Americanization. *American Quarterly,* 52(3), 444-477.

Buck-Morss, S., & Benjamin, W. (1991). *The dialectics of seeing.* Cambridge, MA: MIT Press.

Burdett, R. (2006). Cities: people, society, architecture: 10th international architecture exhibition—Venice Biennale. Retrieved November 27, 2009, from http://www. we-make-money-not-art.com/archives/2007/08/global-cities-a.php.

Cinar, A., & Bender, T. (2007). *Urban imaginaries: Locating the modern city.* Minneapolis, MN: University of Minnesota Press.

De Baan, C., Declerck, J., Patteeuw, V., Sigler, J., & Frausto, S. (2007). *Visionary power: Producing the contemporary city.* Rotterdam, The Netherlands: NAi Publishers.

Ewing, R., Handy, S., Brownson, R. C., Clemente, O., & Winston, E. (2006). Identifying and measuring urban design qualities related to walkability. *Journal of Physical Activity and Health,* 3(Supp 1), 223-240.

Forsyth, A. N. N., & Crewe, K. (2009). New visions for suburbia: Reassessing aesthetics and place-making in modernism, imageability and new urbanism. *Journal of Urban Design,* 14(4), 415-438.

Foster, H. (1995). The artist as ethnographer? The traffic in culture: Refiguring art and anthropology. In *The return of the real* (302-309). Cambridge, MA: MIT Press.

Globalization and World Cities Research Network. (2009). Retrieved November 26, 2009, from http://www.lboro.ac.uk/gawc/.

Gluck, M. (2003). The flâneur and the aesthetic appropriation of urban culture in mid-19th-century Paris. *Theory, Culture & Society,* 20(5), 53-80.

Harvey, D. (2003). *Paris, capital of modernity.* Oxford, UK: Routledge.

Isaacs, R. (2000). The urban picturesque: An aesthetic experience of urban pedestrian places. *Journal of Urban Design,* 5(2), 145-180.

Koepping, K. P. (2005). The fieldworker as performative flâneur: Some thoughts on postmodernism and the transfiguration of doing anthropology. *Zeitschrift für ethnologie,* 130(1), 1-22.

Morris, B. (2004). What we talk about when we talk about 'Walking in the city'. *Cultural Studies,* 18(5), 675-697.

Nylund, K. (2001). Cultural analyses in urban theory of the 1990s. *Acta Sociologica,* 44(3), 219-230.

Parsons, D. (2000). *Streetwalking the metropolis: Women, the city and modernity.* Oxford, UK: Oxford University Press.

Pile, S. (2005). *Real cities: Modernity, space and the phantasmagorias of city life.* New York, NY: Sage.

Seigworth, G., & Gardiner, M. (2004). Rethinking everyday life. *Cultural Studies*, 18(2/3), 139-159.

Short, J. R. (2005). *Imagined country: Environment, culture, and society*. Syracuse, NY: Syracuse University Press.

Short, J. R. (2006). *Urban theory: A critical assessment*. Basingstroke, UK: Palgrave Macmillan.

Solnit, R. (2001). *Wanderlust: A history of walking*. New York, NY: Penguin Group USA.

Tester, K. (1994). *The flâneur*. Oxford, UK: Routledge.

Wolff, J. (2000). The feminine in modern art: Benjamin, Simmel and the gender of modernity. *Theory, Culture, & Society. 17*(6), 33-53.

Qu'implique flâner au féminin en ce début de vingt et unième siècle? Réflexions d'une ethnographe à l'œuvre sur la place de Catalogne à Barcelone

Nadja Monnet

Laboratoire Architecture/Anthropologie (LAA) de l'École Nationale Supérieure d'Architecture de la Villette, Paris.

Abstract

While undertaking an ethnography of a public square in Barcelona, I have been led to wonder about the figure of the flâneur and the difficulties of conceiving this figure in the feminine. Two theories about urban space are in conflict: one views public space as continuing the patriarchy of private space; the other sees public space as a site of freedom and self-development for women as well as men. This same tension is present in analyses of the figure of the flâneur, a figure often evoked when anthropologists work in urban contexts.

Flânerie et ethnographie

Flâner, c'est se balader, sans hâte, en se laissant guider par le hasard des circonstances et des événements du moment. Avec Régine Robin (2009), flâneuse des mégapoles contemporaines, c'est arpenter la ville dans tous les sens, et au moyen de différents moyens de locomotion, pour la saisir pleinement. Réaliser une ethnographie en contexte urbain, c'est partir en quête d'urbanité, se transformer en quelque sorte en un glaneur ou une glaneuse d'indices pour comprendre ce qui fait ville. Pour cerner pleinement et attentivement les dynamiques urbaines, de plus en plus de chercheurs en sciences sociales revendiquent la marche comme une technique. La différence entre le passant ou la passante et l'ethnographe se situe alors au niveau de l'attention portée aux détails et à la qualité des flux, ainsi qu'à l'importance donnée aux agitations urbaines qui se déroulent, sous leurs yeux, sur la voie publique. L'ethnologue s'apparenterait ainsi à la figure du flâneur, largement popularisée par, Edgar Allan Poe, Charles Baudelaire puis Walter Benjamin, ce personnage qui passe son temps à observer la vie citadine. Baudelaire en a fait la quintessence de la métropole moderne en le dépeignant comme un observateur itinérant, qui contemple, sans y participer, l'effervescence urbaine. C'est l'héritier de l'homme des foules d'Edgar Allan Poe, une figure anonyme, perdue au milieu de la foule, qui observe tout sans être observé, un spectateur qui jouit partout de son anonymat. Il est celui qui cherche un refuge dans la foule.

Comme nous le rappelle son étymologie[1], la flânerie est étroitement liée à la naissance des nouvelles urbs du 19ème siècle et plus particulièrement au Paris de cette époque. Depuis, les errances urbaines ont connu différentes mutations. Selon le découpage proposé par Berenstein (2006 : 108-116), elles se divisent en trois moments: la période des flâneries (mi 19ème, début 20ème), l'époque des déambulations (1910-1930) avec les mouvements dadaïste et surréaliste, finalement, celle des dérives (1950-1960) avec les situationnistes et leur critique radicale de l'urbaniste moderne. Avec l'avènement des mégapoles et leur rythme frénétique, l'errance banale, sans intention esthétique, semble devenir difficile. Le nouveau tempo des mégalopoles actuelles empêcherait-il la flânerie? Plus de temps donc pour des échanges furtifs avec les inconnu/es que l'on croiserait dans des espaces qui s'apparenteraient non plus à des rues mais à des surfaces, des esplanades, des centres commerciaux? Le passant et la passante ou les errant/es se seraient transformés en des anonymes traversant des lieux indifférenciés? Le cyberespace serait-il devenu le refuge de la flânerie? Ce n'est pas l'avis de Régine Robin (2009) qui croit que l'acte de flâner est encore réalisable et le met en pratique dans diverses mégalopoles (New York, Los Angeles, Tokyo, Buenos Aires et Londres). Cette auteure reconnaît cependant que cette pratique s'est considérablement modifiée et qu'en fonction des époques des dispositifs différents ont été mis en œuvre pour réinventer la déambulation, la traversée des mégapoles, pour transformer notre regard, notre rapport à la ville, pour piéger nos habitudes, nos horaires, nos parcours obligés. Ainsi parmi les post—flâneurs, comme elle les qualifie, elle distingue clairement entre la pratique de Guy Debord, témoin des transformations urbaines de Paris à la fin des années cinquante, début des années soixante, de celles de Francis Alÿs, Stalker et Bruce Bégout qui prennent la métropole dans toute sa dimension, son hétérogénéité, ses disparités, son hybridité. Robin (2009: 101-102) distingue également entre flânerie et nomadisme. Pour elle, tout oppose le nomade circulant dans son automobile au flâneur qui se faufile dans les rues compactes et denses des villes européennes. Ce dernier, écrit-elle (Robin, 2009:101), « même s'il joue de l'étrangeté, de la distance, de l'air blasé comme le disait Simmel, se trouve en fait toujours dans un environnement familier dont il voudrait se défaire. La rue est son lieu d'élection. Il est chez lui quoi qu'il en dise.» Loin du savoir raffiné du flâneur, elle considère le nomade comme un « analphabète urbain » (Robin, 2009 :102). Il ne fait que transiter dans la ville. C'est la personne toujours en partance, la mobilité pure, celle qui n'est nulle part chez elle. Ce n'est donc pas seulement le tissu urbain qui a changé mais les conditions de possibilité de la flânerie et de sa mémoire.

> « Le flâneur continue de se perdre dans les villes, car on se perd encore dans le labyrinthe des villes. On peut même, luxe suprême, y perdre son temps. Les passants, les artistes et les écrivains, accompagnés de l'ombre des sans-abri, ont mis au point des dispositifs complexes [. . .] pour faire que nous puissions simplement y trouver une place sans nous y installer » (Robin, 2009 :89).

À ces différentes catégories de flâneurs mentionnées par Robin (qui ne consacre que des notes en bas de page aux flâneuses, lorsqu'elle en analyse les différents types[2]), j'y ajouterais une certaine pratique de l'anthropologie évoquée plus haut: des ethnologues qui travaillent en contexte urbain et qui décident, par exemple, de « planter leur tente »[3] sur une place publique, en ne se limitant pas à faire des entretiens au cours de leur terrain mais qui réalisent une écoute et une observation attentive du milieu dans lequel ils/elles se meuvent. Ces anthropologues transforment leur pratique du terrain en un véritable corps à corps avec la ville. Le corps physique du/ de la chercheur/e touche et rencontre alors celui du corps urbain dans les espaces publics de la ville (Berenstein, 2006 :116). Tout comme le flâneur était au seuil de la rue, de la société, de deux époques, à la fois dans la foule et en même temps séparé d'elle (Robin, 2009 : 84-85), l'ethnographe est au seuil de deux mondes, dans une position ambiguë, à la fois angoissante et enivrante. L'anthropologue urbain/e connaît généralement bien l'espace qu'il/elle étudie pour lui être familier et il/elle doit donc réaliser un véritable exercice de défamiliarisation. Elle/Il transforme forcément les dynamiques du milieu qu'elle/il observe tout comme ce dernier l'interpelle et lui demande de se repositionner constamment par rapport à ces idées initiales. On ne sort pas indemne d'un travail de terrain, tout comme le terrain se modifie en présence de l'ethnographe. Car, lorsque l'on fait une « observation flottante » (Pétonnet, 1982) ou que l'on pratique ce qu'Urbain a nommé l' «insu ethnographique» sur une place publique, on ne fait pas qu'observer. On participe pleinement au tableau que l'on tente de dépeindre. Pour éviter la myopie, il s'agit de devenir un/e observateur incorporé/e dont la métamorphose le/la situe au-delà de l'observation participante et, simulation oblige, toujours en deçà de l'identification et de la fusion (Urbain, 2003 : 38-39).

Il s'agit donc d'une question de présence à soi modifiée qui ne peut ignorer les profondes inégalités entre les sexes qui se sont imposées dans les possibilités d'usages des espaces publics urbains. Un espace public n'est pas un espace accessible à tous et à toutes contrairement aux idées reçues. Une sélection, faite de manière plus ou moins tacite, permet à certaines personnes ou à certains groupes de s'approprier ou non les lieux publics. L'espace public n'est pas un simple espace libre, un simple dégagement ou prolongement de l'espace privé du logement, ni même un espace collectif appropriable par une communauté de voisinage. Sa vocation égalitaire, son principe d'accessibilité qui en théorie le régit, est loin d'être une réalité dans la pratique. Tout le monde n'y est pas admis de la même manière. Certain/es peuvent en jouir plus librement que d'autres. La sphère publique n'est pas un espace de et pour tous.

La nature sexuée des espaces publics

> « L'espace est un doute » écrivait Perec (1974). L'espace n'existe pas «en soi». Il est constamment construit, par des pratiques et des programmes d'actions (de la marche aux projets urbanistiques), ou par des discours et des représentations figuratives ou symboliques (l'imaginaire). Il est pensé, interprété et imaginé en même temps qu'habité, vécu ou subi. On sait, notamment depuis les travaux de Piaget (1964), que l'espace est un produit social qui doit être appris. Mais, comme le souligne Barbichon (1991), il est aussi imposé. L'espace public, nous dit-il, n'est pas neutre et les conflits en son sein révèlent des pactes latents. L'espace est préparé par la pratique pour contenir des objets, des relations sociales, des symboles. L'espace n'a de sens que par rapport aux groupes qui l'utilisent. Il est toujours particularisé, orienté, modelé, construit par la collectivité.

Dans certains lieux, notamment les lieux publics, les interactions engendrent donc des « exclusions catégorielles que ce soit en termes d'âge, d'ethnicité, de nationalité, ou d'innombrables autres appartenances catégorielles manifestées publiquement » (Watson, cité par Lieber 2006, note 6). Les lieux sont donc des combinaisons d'espace, de temps (car l'espace implique toujours le temps) et d'un « nous », c'est-à-dire des usagers qui les emploient. Ce sont les relations sociales, les conduites qui constituent l'espace et le temps. Temps et espace sont indissociablement liés. Cependant il ne s'agit pas du temps et de l'espace en tant qu'entités figées mais en tant qu'espace et temps sociaux, c'est-à—dire en fonction de leurs constructions particulières que les sociétés humaines ont élaborées.

On peut donc plausiblement penser que la forme actuelle de nos villes occidentales dépend de la division public/privé qui s'est progressivement imposée depuis la fin du 17ème siècle. Les espaces urbains auraient toujours été différenciés mais avec la révolution industrielle et l'urbanisation accélérée, des changements radicaux se seraient produits au sein des villes occidentales[4]. Elles se seraient zonifiées et seraient devenues plus complexes d'un point de vue spatial, avec la stricte séparation des fonctions et le début des banlieues à grandes échelles. Parallèlement à ces phénomènes, les rôles masculins et féminins se seraient nettement différenciés, reléguant les femmes à la sphère domestique. C'est à partir de la fin du 18ème siècle que les femmes ont vu leur liberté de mouvement se restreindre et se sont transformées en « femmes au foyer », phénomènes qui se systématisent au cours du 19ème siècle. C'est également à ce moment-là qu'il s'insère au mieux dans la cohérence de l'organisation sociale. Les divisions spatiales du public et du privé auraient alors été de plus en plus clairement associées à des spheres considérées comme « naturelles » de chacun des deux sexes, construites sur la base de l'idée de la supériorité, de la domination masculine et de la responsabilité féminine pour la sphère domestique (Moller – Okin, 2000 :374). Il semblerait donc que si la dichotomie public versus privé avait été autre, l'aspect et l'organisation de la vie urbaine seraient certainement bien différente[5].

Il faut néanmoins nuancer ce panorama, car les femmes n'ont pas attendu d'être incluses dans le monde du travail pour réapparaître dans l'espace public. Elles n'en ont d'ailleurs jamais complètement disparu. Si l'idéologie bourgeoise de la première décennie du 19ème siècle, enferment les femmes à la maison, cela ne signifie pas qu'elles n'en sortaient pas Elles le faisaient particulièrement pour réaliser les tâches domestiques (laver le linge, aller au marché, etc.). Cependant leur présence n'était pas synonyme de visibilité. Elles se rendaient dans des lieux publics pour mieux servir la famille. Leur légitimité dans l'espace pouvait seulement être circonscrite à l'espace destiné à la famille: l'espace résidentiel.

Au tournant du 19ème siècle, Simmel faisait déjà l'hypothèse que les femmes ont un autre rapport à l'espace que les hommes; différence qu'il considérait résulter autant de leur « propre nature psycho-physique et supra-historique » que du conditionnement de leurs activités à l'espace de la maison, puisque, pour lui, « les gestes d'un être humain sont dépendants des espaces dans lesquels il se meut habituellement » (1989 :142). Plus proche de nous, Jacqueline Coutras (1996) écrit que c'est parce qu'il y a séparation entre travail domestique et travail salarié et attribution de l'un aux femmes, de l'autre majoritairement aux hommes qu'ont pu se constituer des espaces-temps distincts, que l'on a pu même penser l'organisation de la ville en fonction de cette distinction, et nommer des catégories d'espaces correspondant à chacune des fonctions.

Manuel Delgado (2007 :227) nous rappelle que les notions mêmes de citadin et citoyen considèreraient, dès leurs origines, la femme comme une anomalie, dont la présence dans la rue serait celle d'un corps toujours étranger, mal adapté aux canons d'une normalité qu'elle déforme. L'imaginaire dominant du début des métropoles dépeignait la rue comme un endroit envahi par des dangers. Dans le contexte d'une misogynie dominante qui attribuait aux femmes une force musculaire inférieure, ainsi qu'une vulnérabilité mentale endémique, si la rue était dangereuse pour l'homme (remplie de rencontres imprévues et imprévisibles, pleines d'hypocrisie), elle l'était encore plus pour la femme qui ne pouvait se déplacer que sous l'œil bienveillant et le bras musclé d'un homme. De plus, les femmes étaient également considérées comme moins capables d'éviter les pièges d'un monde d'apparences et de simulacres de par leur « nature » frivole et légère. La rue représentait donc un véritable danger pour tout être féminin, tel que le laissent entrevoir les manuels de savoir-vivre de l'époque[6]. De cette idéologie découle la connotation péjorative du terme « femme publique » qui n'est pas exactement l'équivalent de son homologue masculin. Elle est « un personnage qui d'une certaine façon incarne une irrégularité à corriger: elle est là seule, face au monde, dans l'attente d'être accompagnée, puis accompagnée par cet homme qu'elle attend et, d'une certaine manière, qu'elle convoque, puisque sa présence signale un vide qui n'est autre que celui de l'homme qui devrait être « naturellement » à ses côtés » (Delgado, 2007 :226[7]). Une femme publique est donc supposée être accessible à tous. Pour décrire son contraire, Delgado (2007 : 226-227) suggère le terme de « femme privée » ; ce qui ne signifie pas que ce soit une femme qui jouit d'une vie privée, mais plutôt d'une femme qui est la propriété privée d'un homme et qui lui est exclusive. L'homme public, par contre, est celui qui s'expose (dans le double sens de celui qui est visible et de celui qui sait prendre des risques) aux relations sociales dans un monde d'inconnus, relations qui se basent sur l'apparence et la mise à distance. L'homme public se donne, s'offre au public, ce qui le renvoie du côté du politique, du professionnel dont la grandeur et la qualité de sa réputation dépend du regard et de la valorisation d'autrui. « L'apparent paradoxe qui veut qu'un même attribut (de la rue) hisse l'homme à la catégorie de citoyen et rabaisse la femme à celui de prostituée, ne peut être sans lien avec la manière de concevoir la ville moderne » (Delgado, 2007 :227).

Selon cette perspective, un flâneur ne pouvait être qu'un homme, tous comme les autres " héros" de la ville moderne (l'étranger, l'émigré) qui partagent avec lui la perspective et la possibilité du voyage en solitaire, du déracinement volontaire et l'arrivée anonyme dans un nouvel espace. Contrairement à cette vision des choses, Elizabeth Wilson (1991 :56) ne considère pas le flâneur comme un modèle de masculinité. Ce serait plutôt une figure de la transgression. Il s'agirait d'un être sexuellement non défini, un spectateur passif soit exactement le contraire de l'active participation associée au masculin. Son intérêt pour sa tenue vestimentaire et pour les emplettes ferait du flâneur un être inquiétant de masculinité féminisée. Wilson s'oppose ainsi à la supposée impossibilité de la flâneuse ou à l'association qui fait du flâneur au féminin une prostituée. D'après elle, les femmes, tant au 19ème comme au 20ème siècle, jouirent et continuent de jouir d'une liberté beaucoup plus grande que ce qu'on veut nous faire croire, car au sein des grandes métropoles, les hiérarchies des petites villes ou celles qui régissent les campagnes se diluent; ce qui permet également aux femmes d'expérimenter le déracinement et la liberté de mouvement qu'incarnent les grandes villes. La femme aurait été autant protégée par l'anonymat que l'homme au milieu de la foule. Ce qui lui aurait permis également d'explorer à sa manière le panorama urbain.

Et c'est là peut-être que réside le problème: quelle est cette manière «typique-ment » féminine d'appréhender l'urbain? Car, comme le souligne Janet Wolff (1985), la sociologie moderne ne s'est pas occupée des expériences des femmes dans la vie urbaine[8]. Elle considère que l'abondante littérature sur la nature fugace et transitoire des rencontres types des métropoles urbaines ne correspondent pas à la majorité des expériences féminines. Quelles sont donc ces expériences féminines? Et comment sont-elles vécues?

Une flâneuse-ethnologue sur une place publique

Sans prétention de résoudre cette énigme, je me propose de présenter ci-dessous quelques réflexions qui proviennent de l'observation intensive de la place de

Catalogne à Barcelone et qui, je l'espère, suggéreront quelques éléments de réponses à ce questionnement. Personnellement, je n'avais que rarement traversé cette place, avant de commencer mon travail de terrain, malgré le fait qu'elle soit considérée comme le lieu le plus emblématique de la ville de Barcelone. Pour toute personne qui fréquente la ville, cette place est un passage obligé et immédiatement associée au cœur même de la ville. Les prospectus touristiques ou diverses sources de renseignements destinées aux citadins vantent les mérites de sa centralité et de sa position stratégique. Dans ceux-ci, la Place de Catalogne est décrite comme le centre névralgique de la ville tant sur le plan financier que sur le plan social. Quant aux habitants de la ville, ils s'accordent à dire qu'elle est le centre même de l'activité urbaine, le noyau non seulement physique—c'est d'ailleurs de là que partent les principaux axes de la ville (Les Ramblas, le boulevard Gràcia)—mais également représentatif de la vie citadine entendue dans sa globalité. C'est néanmoins une place que bon nombre d'habitant/es de la ville contourne pour ne pas devoir monter et descendre les quelques marches qui la surélève de ses trottoirs adjacents. À cet obstacle architectonique s'ajoute le fait que ce n'est pas un lieu de rendez-vous habituel dans la cartographie barcelonaise. Des bars, bouches de métro ou une fontaine proche de la place sont des endroits plus prisés pour se retrouver. Le témoignage d'une jeune touriste nous explique son malaise en attente sur la place, malaise assez semblable d'ailleurs à mes premières visites, au cours desquelles je me sentais complètement déplacée et ne savais pas très bien comment gérer mes déplacements sur la place :

> «C'est vraiment pas un endroit pour attendre quelqu'un. Tu ne sais pas où te mettre. Si tu attends au milieu, tu te sens bête. T'as l'impression que tu t'exposes à la vue de tous. Si tu t'installes sur un banc, il y a le risque que les personnes avec qui tu as rendez—vous ne te voient pas, en plus, sur quels bancs? La première rangée passe encore mais les bancs de derrière, ils ont l'air vraiment glauques. Ils donnent pas confiance. Moi, je ne m'y assoirai pas. J'ai vraiment passé un mauvais quart d'heure sur cette place. C'est pas un lieu ou je redonnerai rendez-vous à quelqu'un ».

Pour tenter de rendre compte des différentes dynamiques de la place, j'y suis pourtant revenue régulièrement, au minimum deux heures par jour pendant 6 mois (d'avril à septembre 2005), puis de manière plus sporadique depuis[9]. J'ai commencé par l'apprivoiser en m'asseyant d'abord sur ses bancs et en explorant ses différents coins et recoins. Ce n'est que bien plus tard, lorsqu'elle m'était déjà suffisamment familière, que je me suis aventurée à m'installer sur ses pelouses. Cela a été comme la redécouvrir sous un autre angle et j'ai dû répéter l'exercice un bon nombre de fois avant de cesser de me sentir ridicule sur ces espaces verts.

Du point de vue de l'espace, la place s'organise de la manière suivante: trois rangées de bancs s'alignent l'une derrière l'autre et entourent le centre de la place d'un hémicycle, tel qu'on en trouve dans les salles de spectacle. Si les activités qui se réalisent sur ces bancs ne semblent pas fondamentalement différentes, on peut néanmoins remarquer une ambiance quelque peu distincte pour chacune d'elles. La première rangée contient clairement des « spectateurs » qui ne quittent presque jamais du regard, même si ce n'est parfois que de manière distraite, ce qui se déroule devant eux. Le centre de la place est l'espace par excellence de ceux et celles qui veulent se mettre en scène et « se présenter en spectacle ». Nous avons surnommé ces personnes les performers. Les deux autres rangées sont moins propices à ce genre d'exercice, car une fois assis, l'usager ou l'usagère du lieu n'a que rarement une vue plongeante sur la place, celle-ci étant généralement entravée par les buissons qui séparent la première rangée de la deuxième. Ces deux dernières rangées forment, de par leurs caractéristiques, des espaces qui semblent plus intimes et qui favorisent davantage les rencontres, bien que celles-ci puissent également avoir lieu sur les bancs de la première rangée. Les activités délictueuses tendent, quant à elles, à se réaliser dans la troisième rangée et généralement proches d'une « sortie » pour permettre de quitter rapidement le lieu du délit et se fondre dans la foule de piétons avoisinant la place. Peu à peu, j'ai commencé à distinguer parmi le fourmillement de la place, les usagers et usagères habituel/les des visiteurs et visiteuses plus sporadiques ou des passant/es qui la traversent. Parmi les premiers, on peut mentionner les vendeurs et vendeuses à qui appartiennent les quatre stands installés sur la place et qui proposent aux badauds et badaudes des friandises, ballons et autres gadgets. En font partie également lesdifférent/es « technicien/nes » (balayeurs et balayeuses de rue, police, brigade de conservation des monuments, etc.), mais aussi les flâneurs et flâneuses occasionnel/les ou encore les « hommes de la ronde », ainsi dénommés parce qu'ils passent leur temps à se balader en faisant le tour de la place, dans un sens comme dans l'autre.

Les décomptes réalisés in situ, lors du deuxième travail de terrain, ont rapidement confirmé ce que nous avions pu observer intuitivement lors du premier. Moins de personnes de sexe féminin fréquentent ces lieux par rapport à celles de sexe masculin, bien qu'il existent des pointes de fréquentations féminines qui coïncident avec les heures de sorties d'école ou de bureau. Je ferais remarquer au passage que lors des décomptes réalisés sur la place, il n'y a que rarement eu confusion pour déterminer le sexe des corps en présence, même si nous n'avons jamais eu l'idée de vérifier si notre manière de percevoir la chose correspondait à la façon de s'identifier de ces personnes. On peut se poser des questions quant à la pertinence de diviser les usagers en deux groupes, l'un de sexe masculin, l'autre de sexe féminin. Il faut donc avoir à l'esprit les biais possibles d'une telle manière de faire, d'une part, parce que comme Lieber (2006) le souligne, on rencontre, à l'heure actuelle—et depuis l'incorporation des femmes au marché du travail—une certaine unification dans les pratiques de l'espace public et, d'autre part, parce que « la comparaison des différences de genre peut sembler une position épistémologique suspecte, puisqu'elle peut être précédée par l' « incontournable postulat » que les êtres humains sont divisés en deux sexes, et seulement deux, avant de décrire et classifier le comportement de ceux qui ont été ainsi définis par ces catégories dichotomiques » (Kessler, Mac Kenna, cités par Cassell,

2000 :64). Il n'y a pas dans le monde des hommes et des femmes ou des mâles et des femelles en soi, mais uniquement du genre construit à travers des luttes historiques entre des groupes dans des sociétés structurées par classe, race, sexualité, etc. pour l'accès à des ressources sociales (symboliques et matérielles) (Parini, 2006 :33).

Mon intention n'a pas été de réduire les attitudes féminines et masculines à des variables relativement prédictibles, selon un modèle prépondérant, ce qui aurait conduit à appauvrir considérablement le « « tonitruant désordre » de la réalité humaine, des motivations, des comportements des êtres humains » (Cassell, 2000 :61). Néanmoins pour donner sens à mes observations, il a bien fallu organiser ce que j'observais au moyen de catégories, consciente que toute opération de classification consiste à découper arbitrairement dans une réalité aux innombrables possibilités[10]. D'autre part, malgré les tentatives de dépasser les démarcations du féminin et du masculin, malgré les interventions sur les corps qui tentent de se détacher des références biologiques (tel que le queer, le transsexuel, le bisexuel, etc.), les catégories homme/femme semblent persister comme lieu d'énonciation des relations de pouvoir qui opèrent comme des miroirs et reflètent les rapports politiques, économiques et symboliques en vigueur qui octroient une valeur et un statut différents au féminin et au masculin, posant ainsi des bases inégales qui ont ensuite des répercutions dans les différentes sphères de la vie quotidienne où se construisent les subjectivités et les pratiques des sujets. Comme le souligne Teresa Del Valle (1997), la femme occidentale du 21ème siècle ne semble pas encore avoir réussi à se séparer des tâches qui lui sont traditionnellement attribuées. Ses trajets urbains continuent à être fortement influencés par son rôle de « femme au foyer », rôle assumé de plus en plus à temps partiel, à côté des tâches ménagères et des différents soins donnés aux membres de la famill[11]. Les itinéraires féminins se perpétuent et se ressemblent terriblement: le chemin de l'école, celui des courses, etc. Les sorties d'écoles et de garderies, les supermarchés sont encore des espaces avant tout investis par les femmes et à partir desquels celles-ci organisent cognitivement le reste de leur cartes mentales de l'espace urbain.

S'il est difficile de recenser les passantes, j'ai pu constater que les femmes seules n'occupent que rarement les bancs et si c'est le cas, elles ne le restent généralement pas longtemps: soit parce que quelqu'un les rejoint peu de temps après qu'elles s'y soient installées, soit parce qu'elles n'y font qu'une brève pause dans leur parcours qui les mènera ailleurs. Lorsque les femmes sont seules sur la place, elles sont généralement peu loquaces. Il semble, en effet, qu'une norme tacite considèrerait qu'une femme seule n'en aborde pas une autre, dans la même situation, pour engager une conversation de longue durée, sans créer un certain malaise, semblable à celui qu'un homme abordant une femme seule peut provoquer. Tout semble mis en œuvre pour que les femmes non accompagnées doivent demander une « autorisation de séjour » en ces lieux, une autorisation qui se concrétise à travers différentes justifications qu'elles se sentent obligées de donner pour pouvoir rester un moment sur la place ou pouvoir engager la conversation avec quelqu'un. Une demande d'information, l'attente d'un/e ami/e ou d'un parent, le goûter des enfants, le besoin d'accompagner leur mari (dans le cas de femmes âgées) ou une personne dont on est chargée de s'occuper sont autant d'excuses utilisées pour justifier leur présence dans cet espace dynamique dont seule la gent masculine semble profiter pleinement. Les hommes n'ont pas besoin de prétexte, personne ne leur demande d'explications en leur jetant des regards interrogateurs. Apparemment, ils peuvent y rester, comme bon leur semble, sans rien y faire voire même y réaliser des transactions peu fiables, sans avoir besoin de s'excuser ni de devoir inventer des prétextes. Ils sont présents et font ce qui leur convient le mieux quand cela les intéresse: se balader, s'asseoir, discuter, aborder les passant/es, etc.

En effet, pour la grande majorité de mes interlocuteurs masculins, l'ethnologue en solo que j'étais, à l'œuvre dans cet espace public, était interprété comme synonyme de disponibilité, de femme facile, en quête d'aventure. Les diverses propositions qui m'ont été faites ou les conversations qui se sont brusquement interrompues lorsque mon statut (mariée avec des enfants) était dévoilé dans la conversation, me l'ont clairement rappelé. Ces gestes et manières d'agir, m'ont rapidement fait comprendre qu'on attendait autre chose de ma part, tout comme les regards perplexes voire inquisiteurs des hommes qui comme moi flânaient sur la place de Catalogne.

Ainsi, bien que les femmes ne soient plus confinées à l'espace domestique, l'identité sexuée joue encore un rôle important lorsque l'on déambule dans l'espace public. Lieber (2006) à la suite notamment de Goffman (1977)[12], rappelle que les femmes ne sont tolérées dans l'espace public que dans certaines circonstances et l'une d'elles, semble-t-il, est de ne pas s'y exposer de n'importe quelle manière et, en tous cas, de ne pas y adopter des attitudes qui sortent des schémas préconçus qu'on attend d'elles. C'est également ce que nous raconte Régine Robin (2009) quand elle nous explique que ses flâneries ont dû être encadrées, organisées, même si elles restaient ouvertes aux imprévus:

> «Traverser les mégapoles, maintenir contre vents et marées la spécificité
> du flâneur, nécessite quelques précautions. Les mégapoles, mêmes celles
> du « premier monde » génèrent la peur. Le fait que je sois une femme entre
> deux âges, pas forcément une touriste mais une étrangère à coup sûr, une
> flâneuse insolite, n'est pas indifférent aux difficultés que je rencontre. Cela
> m'expose, me fragilise. Je dois à tout moment en tenir compte » (p.24)[13].

Il semble donc que le marquage spatial des femmes se traduit par un sabotage du droit de pouvoir jouir des avantages de l'anonymat qui devrait présider les relations entre inconnus dans les espaces publics. La nature neutre et mixte de l'espace public est plus une déclaration de principe qu'une réalité palpable, comme l'est également la supposée promiscuité relationnelle qui aurait lieu en son sein. Paradoxalement, dans la rue, sur une place publique, la même femme qui est «invisibilisée» en tant que sujet social souffre d'une « hypervisibilisation » en tant qu'objet d'attention. Les femmes—ou du moins certaines, considérées comme abordables—sont constamment victimes d'agressions au niveau le plus élémentaire—clin d'œil, interpellations légères, voire grossières, etc.—mais cet excès de focalisation peut également adopter la forme plus subtile de la galanterie. Les femmes savent que l'espace urbain ne leur appartient pas complètement. Elles savent qu'elles peuvent en utiliser certaines parties et à certaines heures. Si elles sont autorisées à y séjourner, c'est en temps qu'invitée et à la condition qu'elles sachent s'y tenir de manière adéquate. C'est certainement la raison pour laquelle, parmi tous les performers observés jusqu'à présent, aucun de sexe féminin n'a été recensé. Il semblerait donc que les femmes ne peuvent pas se permettre d'adopter des attitudes déviantes[14] dans l'espace public sous peine de perdre la face. Si, actuellement, les femmes sont nettement plus présentes dans l'espace public[15], le contexte urbain leur transmet constamment des messages pour qu'elles sachent quelle est leur place[16], car la structure sociale est présente au sein même de toutes interactions et celles-ci semblent encore être beaucoup plus difficiles et risquées pour les femmes que pour les hommes.

Parallèlement à ces micro-situations, j'ai pu aussi constater des manières d'agir de jeunes filles très différentes de celles de leurs aînées. S'asseoir sur les accoudoirs ou le dos des bancs, en petits groupes, par terre, au milieu de la place, les jambes écartées, allongées sur les pelouses, se bécoter en plein jour et à la vue de tous sur les bancs publics ne semblent pas les incommoder. Comme le souligne Jolé (2002 : 114-115), les groupes de jeunes, en agissant de cette manière, sont en train de transformer les postures habituelles. Ils expérimentent de nouvelles manières de faire des pauses dans la ville et d'exposer leurs corps dans l'espace public. Les normes d'usage concernant les manières de se comporter dans l'espace public semblent donc en phase de changement. Certains tabous, certaines barrières ont-ils été rompus ou ces attitudes relèvent-elles d'un âge qui, une fois passé, ne semble pas avoir été au-delà d'une apparente normalité ?

De l'auto-exclusion à l'exploration de postures qui façonnent les lieux

Pendant longtemps les femmes s'auto-excluaient de certains lieux publics, soit parce que leur éducation leur en interdisait l'accès soit parce que quand elles s'y aventuraient elles ne s'y sentaient pas bien reçues. Le témoignage d'Angelina Vilella (2000) de l'Hospitalet (ville attenante à Barcelone) nous l'explique :

> «Aujourd'hui quand on a soif, on entre dans un bar et on commande une eau ou autre chose mais avant c'était impensable, d'abord, parce qu'on n'en avait pas les moyens et ensuite parce que, à cette époque, les dames n'entraient jamais seules dans un bar. C'était mal vu qu'une femme entre sans accompagnant masculin dans un bar public, elle était immédiatement cataloguée. Ce n'est pas avant les années soixante et des poussières que, par chance, la question a commencé à être normalisée. Moi, je me souviens … la première fois que je suis entrée toute seule boire un café au lait dans un bar, c'était en 1965. Je me sentais mal à l'aise, comme si j'avais fait quelque

chose de mal; et je l'avais fait simplement pour ne pas m'endormir en cours. Les copines de classe (de l'école d'infirmerie) qui le faisaient déjà, m'y ont fait entrer » (p.81, traduction personnelle).

Ce que signifie être une femme ou un homme dépend donc du contexte; la définition est relationnel et variable, bien que toujours soumise aux lois et réglementations d'une époque donnée. Toute personne naît dans un système culturel et social qui lui préexiste et qui la détermine partiellement; cependant, malgré le fait que les rôles soient codifiés au départ, les personnes ont une réelle capacité de transgression et de résistance. La polarisation entre les sexes est un fait social qui justifie des inégalités. Si ces inégalités deviennent inacceptables, les discours sur la différence des sexes ont une chance de s'estomper. La «sexuation» de l'espace, si je peux me permettre l'expression, n'arrive pas à dévaluer ni à désactiver complètement les vertus de l'espace public urbain. Le principal avantage de la vie urbaine moderne consiste à permettre aux citadins d'être maître de leurs choix, en se libérant des contraintes communautaires et de la « prison » des traditions. Il est certain qu'actuellement les femmes continuent de bénéficier des effets libérateurs des villes, bien que d'un autre côté elles souffrent des phénomènes d'exclusion économique et sociale. La ville moderne occidentale, plus que de mettre fin au lien qui unit prioritairement (sinon exclusivement) un sexe à l'espace de résidence, l'a assoupli. La ville du 21ème siècle permettra-t-elle de « désexuer » la distinction privé/public, c'est-à-dire de détacher la définition des sphères de celle des rôles sexués?

Le rapport entre espace urbain et possibilité de transgression des versions hégémoniques de la sexualité documentées par les féministes ne concerne d'ailleurs pas que les femmes mais également les hommes. S'introduire dans l'espace public dans le sens que lui donne Hannah Arendt (1974) d'espace où s'expriment et se négocient les différences—entrer sur le marché du travail, participer aux intrigues du pouvoir politique, occuper un espace dans la production et la circulation des signes—suppose de se demander comment le féminin et ses symboles se transforment. De même, le masculin ne reste pas sans être impacté par ces nouvelles manières féminines de transiter. Il se réinterprète et élabore de nouvelles définitions et pratiques. L'émergence de nouvelles valeurs féminines provoque un bouleversement dans les relations traditionnelles hommes-femmes qui déconcertent autant les hommes que les femmes.

Comme le souligne Coutras (1998), on ne peut espérer améliorer l'aménagement de l'espace de façon à rendre la pratique plus équitable, pour les hommes et pour les femmes, et en même temps vouloir le laisser inchangé dans son organisation. Toute modification du rapport des sexes à l'espace aboutit forcément à modifier son fonctionnement. Les espaces, comme les corps, ne sont pas neutres. Les espaces naissent des rapports de pouvoir, les rapports de pouvoir établissent des normes et les normes définissent des limites qui sont aussi bien sociales que spatiales. Mais les espaces dépendent également des usages qui en sont fait. Comme écrit de Certeau (1990 : 142-147), dans la vie quotidienne, l'homme et la femme de la foule vont et viennent, circulent, débordent et se livrent à toutes sortes de dérives sur un relief qui leur est imposé mais dont ils s'accommodent suivant leur propre entendement. Le marcheur ou la marcheuse urbain(e) donne vie à une « ville transhumante ou métaphorique qui s'insinue dans le texte clair de la ville planifiée et lisible » (p. 142). Il/Elle profite des accidents de terrain, s'apparente à son entourage, passant entre les rochers et les dédales des quadrillages institutionnels qu'il/elle érode et déplace et de qui l'ordre officiel ne sait rien ou du moins presque rien. Ses ruses et combinaisons de pouvoirs sans identité lisible, sans prises saisissables, sans transparence rationnelle sont impossibles à gérer. Les jeux de pas sont donc «façonnages d'espace » (p. 147). Ces motricités piétonnières qui spatialisent trament des lieux, précise Michel de Certeau. Cessons donc d'être des invitées et devenons des amphitryonnes!

Mais partons également à la recherche des ruses urbaines féminines qui permettent aux passantes de « « détourner » les architectures et les espaces urbains, et d'inventer des artifices afin de s'approprier et réinventer leur espace » (De Biase, 2006 :91). Car comme avertit Wilson (1991 :10), c'est une erreur d'écrire sur l'hostilité de la ville vis-à-vis des femmes. Insister sur les problèmes de sécurité, de protection, c'est réifier la domination patriarcale, promouvoir le paternalisme.

> « We need a radically new approach to the city. We will never solve the problems of living in the cities until we welcome and maximise the freedom and autonomy they offer and make these available to all classes and groups. We must cease to perceive the city as a dangerous and disorderly zone from which women—and others—must be largely excluded for their protection» (p. 9).

Comme le suggère Laplantine (2005), supplantons les topographies par des chorégraphies qui ont « l'avantage de nous faire comprendre (mais d'abord de nous faire ressentir, regarder, écouter), l'ensemble du chœur qui désigne à la fois le lieu où l'on danse et l'art de danser » (2005 :42). Cet auteur ajoute à la notion de chorégraphie celle de kairos, qu'il définit comme l'instant où on n'est plus avec les autres dans une simple relation de co-existence, mais où on commence à être troublé et transformé par eux.

> « Alors que dans une approche topographique, on prend, on saisit, on s'empare d'un objet, dans une approche chorégraphique, et plus précisément dans le temps du kairos, il n'y a plus d'objets pouvant être considérés comme un dehors radical. Le temps des verbes et les verbes eux-mêmes ne sont plus les mêmes: non plus prendre, saisir, s'emparer de, mais surprendre, être surpris comme dans le duende du flamenco. Kairos est ce moment précis où nous renonçons aux fictions de l' « autre », de l' « étranger » [auquel j'ajouterai du « sexe »] et où nous réalisons une expérience qui est celle de l'étrangeté » (p. 43).

Il s'agit donc de remettre en cause les stéréotypes de la pensée identitaire, spatiale et statique. Sans renoncer à l'analyse, il s'agit de penser le temps, bien que celui-ci ne soit ni divisible, ni ne se répète et qu'il ne permette donc pas des coupes immobilisant le flux du mouvement (Laplantine, 2005 : 43).

Sachons être attentives et attentifs aux « corpographies » (Dultra, Berenstein, 2008[17]) qui mettent en évidence les résistances des corps contre l'hostilité des lieux. Car construire la ville comme terre d'accueil demande une attention aux moindres détails et aux besoins de tous les passants et passantes. En flânant, ne nous lassons pas d'explorer les interstices, les failles, les espaces-temps «inutiles mais nécessairement utilisés», «ces espaces qui ne correspondent à rien dans le Grand Ordre » et qui constituent des trous « dans le tissu des fonctions et des nécessités »[18]. Tentons de comprendre ce que nous dit la danse des corps dans l'espace public et demandons-nous comment ces corps sont en train de changer avec l'accélération généralisée de la mobilité. Scrutons les logiques sociales qui permettent qu'un lieu public soit quelque chose de plus qu'un simple territoire d'accessibilité et de circulation, un réseau de rapports instables entre inconnus ou à peine connus, une prolifération constante et changeante.

Notes

[1] D'après le *Nouveau dictionnaire étymologique et historique* (1964), le mot flâner date du milieu du 17ème siècle (flanner). Ce mot normand, sans doute plus ancien, est vulgarisé au 19ème mais pourrait provenir également du scandinave flana, aller çà et là . Le mot flânerie apparaît au 16ème siècle mais est rarement employé jusqu'au 19ème siècle. En 1856, Furpille invente le néologisme « flânocher ».

[2] Étrangement elle intitule également son ouvrage *Mégapolis; les derniers pas du flâneur* et non de la flâneuse, ce qui peut s'explique par le fait que cette figure, dans la littérature, a été plus masculine que féminine. Ceci n'a cependant pas empêché certaines femmes de se livrer à la flânerie, comme le suggère l'étude de Catherine Nesci, *Le flâneur et les flâneuses; les femmes et la ville à l'époque romantique*. Grenoble : ELLUG/Université Stendhal, 2007.

[3] La « tente », objet-fétiche de l'anthropologue, est une sorte de sanctuaire et, d'une certaine manière, la « chambre noire » de son travail de terrain. C'est d'ailleurs l'objet de la première photographie que Malinowski (considéré comme le père fondateur de l'ethnographie en tant que pratique de terrain) insère dans sa monographie « Les Argonautes du Pacifique » avec la légendesuivante: «La tente de l'ethnographe sur la plage de Nu'agasi. Cela montre la façon de s'installer et de vivre parmi les indigènes . . . » (Samain, 1995 :110, note11).

[4] Certaines auteures émettent même l'hypothèse que l'urbanisation coïnciderait avec une intensification du patriarcat, entendu comme le pouvoir exercé par la gent masculine au sein de la famille (Darke, 1998 :119-122).

[5] Sans vouloir m'attarder davantage sur cette dichotomie public/privé, je voudrais néanmoins souligner que les sphères privées et publiques n'existent pas en elles-mêmes. Ce sont des constructions qui ont une histoire et qui diffèrent en fonction des contextes. Moller-Okin (2000 :372) précise que les concepts dupublic et du domestique ont non seulement servi à organiser la vie sociale de manière différente selon les périodes historiques (la production,

par exemple, est totalement passée de la sphère domestique à la sphère publique, en l'espace des derniers trois cents ans) mais ils ont également eu des connotations très différentes (comme l'intimité, par exemple, qui ne fut perçue comme une caractéristique de la sphère privée qu'à partir de la fin du 17ème siècle).

6   Le message indirect que ces manuels transmettaient à leurs lectrices pour qu'elles ne s'exposent pas et ne perdent pas leur réputation en s'engageant dans l'espace public, était que les femmes devaient « se protéger de cet espace en l'évitant et en laissant le champ libre aux hommes qui savaient mieux en juguler les risques » (Coutras, 1996 :107). Pour plus de détails, se référer à J. Coutras « Bienséance, moralité et rapport de sexes appliqués à l'espace» in: G. Zanotto, *Le langages des représentations géographiques*. Univerité degli Studi di Venezia, Venise, 1989, vol.2, p. 235-250.

7   Traduction personnelle et ajout de guillemets.

8   Coutras (1991 :98) souligne également que les descriptions et analyses d'interactions dans l'espace public par des auteurs qui se réclament de R. Park, G. Simmel, L. Wirth ou G. Tarde mettent en scène des personnes asexuées et les dénominations pour les caractériser (l'étranger, le noctambule, l'aventurier, etc.) sont toujours au masculin. Néanmoins, pour cette auteure, ces faits relèvent d'une logique intrinsèque à l'espace urbain, puisque pour elle "les personnages de la ville intersubjective sont bien uniquement masculins" (Coutras, 1991 :99).

9   Ces réflexions sont le fruit de deux recherches. La première s'est déroulée d'avril 2005 à février 2006, avec un projet intitulé « Au cœur de la Ville: Analyse du pouls de la Place de Catalogne » pour lequel María Isabel Tovar et moi-même avons obtenu une aide à la recherche, octroyée par l'Inventaire du Patrimoine Ethnologique de Catalogne (IPEC) du Département de la Culture du Gouvernement catalan. Pour plus de précisions concernant cette première phase de recherche, se référer à Monnet (2007 et sous presse). Un deuxième projet de recherche, intitulé « Espace urbain et genre en contexte méditerranéen: Parcours sonores et—photographiques des usagers de la Place de Catalogne à Barcelone », avec une perspective genre plus clairement définie, également financé par l'IPEC et pour lequel j'ai aussi obtenu un subside pour la recherche de l'École Doctorale Lémanique en Études Genre, est en cours de réalisation, depuis février 2008.

10 L'image que propose Lévi-Strauss, dans *La Pensée Sauvage*, est très suggestive à cet égard. Pour expliquer ce qui se passe lorsque nous classifions, il utilise l'image d'un filet qui se pose sur le monde, ce qui permet « d'attraper » d'expliquer certaines choses mais en laisse d'autres à l'extérieur. Ainsi toute opération de classification est une sélection qui appauvrit la diversité des possibles, en fonction d'un but précis.

11 Une étude récente de Cristina Carrasco Begoña et Mònica Serrano Gutiérrez (2006) dévoile qu'en Catalogne, actuellement, 71,7% des tâches ménagères et familiales sont réalisées par des femmes.

12 Dans ce court texte (2002 [1977]), Goffman met en évidence les mécanismes de la naturalisation dans l'espace public de la dichotomie homme/femme, ainsi que la construction de cette idéologie de la nature. C'est-à-dire qu'il démontre par des exemples concrets que le genre et le sexe ne sont pas des faits dérivés d'un simple ordre naturel mais qu'ils sont susceptibles d'être construits et recréés. Ces notions appartiennent à l'ordre symbolique, à

l'idéologie, même si ensuite les énoncés de cet ordre symbolique proposent de les instituer comme des faits naturels pour tous les membres de la société. Ainsi, par exemple, son analyse de l'institution des toilettes séparées pour les hommes et pour les femmes montre qu'il s'agit d'un dispositif qui relève d'un phénomène culturel, rien n'exigeant physiologiquement que le dispositif soit différent pour les uns et pour les autres. Il en conclut que «la ségrégation des toilettes est présentée comme une conséquence naturelle de la différence entre les classes sexuelles, alors qu'en fait c'est plutôt un moyen d'honorer, sinon de produire, cette différence » (2002 :82). Les rôles sexués ne découlent donc pas «naturellement» des différences biologiques mais sont le résultat de constructions sociales.

[13] Pour éviter ce type de problème, George Sand se déguise en homme pour pouvoir flâner à loisir (Wilson, 1991 :52).

[14] L'emploi du terme déviant n'est pas à comprendre dans son acception négative, mais dans le sens d'un comportement qui s'écarte de la norme sociale admise du groupe d'appartenance.

[15] L'augmentation du nombre de femmes qui circulent librement dans la ville ne daterait pas d'hier mais du milieu du 19ème siècle, selon Wilson (1991), et serait due à la création de nouveaux postes de travail que suscitent les grands-magasins et, que, d'autre part, les femmes pouvaient fréquenter seules pour y faire des emplettes ou du lèche-vitrine.

[16] Notons au passage et avec Darke (1998 :117) que pour certains hommes également la ville est inhospitalière. Ne jouissant pas d'une pleine reconnaissance de la part de l'ordre public patriarcal, ils ne peuvent pas non plus s'exposer de n'importe quelle manière dans l'espace urbain.

[17] Ces deux auteures incitent à réfléchir sur les rapports possibles entre corps et ville qu'elles ont nommé corpographies et qu'elles différencient clairement de la cartographie et des chorégraphies. Pour elles, l'étude des corpographies peut contribuer à remettre en question les phénomènes d'esthétisation et de spectacularisation des villes auxquels nous assistons. « Un véritable dialogue entre architecture, urbanisme, arts et danse permettra de comprendre les liens contemporains existants entre corps, arts, ambiance et ville, ce qui permettra de promouvoir un regard critique sur la manière dont ces notions évoluent dans la pratique et les discours produits par les différentes disciplines de la connaissance» (p.85, traduction personnelle).

[18] Les parties entre guillemets sont des extraits de la voix off du film de Yaël André (2007), film par ailleurs très suggestif qui présente des corpographies de gestes quotidiens et qui interroge les limites de l'esprit cartographique. Un clin d'œil, plein d'espoir, à la puissance et l'impuissance de l'ordre et du chaos humains.

Références

André, Yaël (2007). Chats errants, *Zones temporaires d'inutilité, Belgique*, 56" [DVD].

Arendt, Hannah (1993 [1974]). *La condición humana,* Barcelona, Buenos Aires, Méico: Ed. Paidos. [Titre original: The Human Condition].

Barbichon, Guy (1991). « Espaces partagés: variation et variété des cultures », *Espaces et sociétés*, no 62-63, 107-133.

Berenstein, Paola (2006). «Errances urbaines: l'art de faire l'expérience de la vie; Autres chemins contre la spectacularisation urbain» in: Pierre-Henry Jeudy, Paola Berenstein (eds.). *Corps et décors urbains: les enjeux culturels des villes.* Paris : L'Harmattan, 103-116.

Booth, Chris, Darke, Jane et Llenadle, Susan (eds.) (1998). *La vida de las mujeres en las ciudades; la ciudad, un espacio para el cambio,* Madrid: Narcea. [Titre original: Changing Places; Women's Lives in the City].

Carrasco Begoña, Cristina et Serrano Gutiérrez, Mònica (2006).*Compte satèl·lit de la producció domèstica de les llars de Catalunya* 2001, Barcelona: Institut Català de les Dones.

Cassell, Joan (2000). « Différence par corps: les chirurgiennes », *Cahiers du Genre,* no 29, 53-81.

Coutras, Jacqueline (1996). *Crise urbaine et espaces sexués,* Paris: Armand Colin. Coutras, Jacqueline (1998). *Construction sexuée de l'espace urbain: le devoir spatial des femmes,* http://www.habiter—autrement.org/22_sex/03_genre.htm (consulté le 28 décembre 2007).

Darke, Jane (1998). La ciudad modelada por el varón, In: Chris Booth, Jane Darke et Susan Llenadle (eds.). *La vida de las mujeres en las ciudades; la ciudad, un espacio para el cambio,* Madrid: Narcea, 116-130.

De Biase, Alessia (2006). Ruses urbaines comme savoir, In: Pierre—Henry Jeudy, Paola Berenstein (eds.). *Corps et décors urbains; les enjeux culturels des villes.* Paris: L'Harmattan, 91-100.

De Certeau, Michel (1990 [1980]). Marches dans la ville, in: Michel de Certeau. *L'invention du quotidien.* 1. Arts de faire, Paris: Gallimard, 139-191.

Delgado, Manuel (2007). *Ciudades movedizas,* Barcelona: Anagrama.

Del Valle, Teresa (1997). *Andamios para una nueva ciudad; lecturas desde la antropología,* Madrid: Cátedra; Valencia: Universitat de València : Instituto de la Mujer.

Dultra Britto, Fabiana et Berenstein Jacques, Paola (2008). « Cenografias e corpografias urbanas, um diálogo sobre as relações entre corpo e cidade», Cadernos PPG-AU FAUFBA, ano VI, número especial: Paisagens do corpo, 79-86.

Goffman, Erving (2002 [1977]). *L'arrangement des sexes,* Paris: La Dispute.

Jolé, Michèle (2002). « Quand la ville invite à s'asseoir; le banc public parisien et la tentative de la dépose », *Les Annales de la recherche urbaine,* no 94, décembre, 107-115.

Laplantine, François (2005). *Le social et le sensible: introduction à une anthropologie modale,* Paris: Téraèdre.

Lieber, Marylène (2006). « Les peurs dans l'espace public, l'apport d'une réflexion sur le genre des violences », in: Emmanuel *Gleyze. Peurs et risques contemporains. Une approche pluridisciplinaire,* Paris: L'Harmattan.

Mc Dowell, Linda (2000 [1999]). *Género, identidad y lugar; un estudio de las geografías feministas,* Madrid: Cátedra. [Titre original: Gender, Identity and Place; Understanding Feminist Geographies].

Moller-Okin, Susan (2000). « Le genre, le public et le privé », in: Thanh-Huyen Ballmer-Cao, Véronique Mottier et Léa Sgier (eds.). *Genre et politique: Débats et perspectives, Paris:* Gallimard, Folio Essais, 345-396.

Monnet, Nadja (2007). La Ciudad, instrucciones de uso; esbozos barceloneses. Thèse de doctorat, Université de Barcelone, Département d'Anthropologie Sociale. http://www.tesisenxarxa.net/TDX-1010107-130510/

Monnet, Nadja (sous presse). «Confrontations d'enjeux et d'usages sur la Place de Catalogne », in: Alessia De Biase; Monica Coralli et Jean François Tibillon (eds). *Espaces en commun*, Lyon: Certu.

Parini, Lorena (2006). Le système de genre: introduction aux concepts et théories, Zürich: Ed. Seismos.

Perec, Georges (2000 [1974]). *Espèce d'espaces*, Paris: Galilée. Pétonnet, Colette (1982). "L'observation flottante: l'exemple d'un cimetière Parisien," *L'Homme* (Paris) 22 (4), 1982, 37-47.

Piaget, Jean (1964). *L'Épistémologie génétique de l'espace*, Paris: PUF.

Robin, Régine (2009). *Mégapolis: les derniers pas du flâneur*, Paris: Stock.

Samain, Étienne (1995). «Bronislaw Malinowski et la photographie anthropologique», *L'Ethnographie* (Paris), 1995, t. 91 (2), no 118, 107-130.

Simmel, Georg (1989). *Philosophie de la modernité: la femme, la ville, l'individualisme,* Paris: Payot, vol. 1.

Urbain, Jean-Didier (2003). *Ethnologue, mais pas trop*. Paris: Payot, Petite bibliothèque.

Vilella, Angelina (2000). *Jo . . . també recordo*, L'Hospitalet: Ateneu popular de l'Hospitalet.

Wilson, Elizabeth (1991). *The Sphinx in the City*, Londres: Virago.

Wolff, Janet (1985). The invisible flâneuse: women and the literature of modernity, *Theory, Culture and Society*, no 2, 37-46.

The Nomadic Experiment of a Steppe Land Flâneuse

Dianne Chisholm

University of Alberta

Abstract

Imagine the flâneuse in Ulaanbataar, with its streets unnavigable for pedestrians, and its ever-shifting ger neighborhoods that abut onto crumbling Gulag architecture, not to mention its fierce resurrection of Genghis Khan whose portrait engraved into the overlooking hills declares the city's imperious nomadic autonomy. This paper investigates the mobilization of the 21st-century flâneuse by the contrary material forces of nomadism and urbanism that confront and transform her as she stumbles, drifts and speeds through Mongolia's city and steppes. The focus of investigation concerns the (im)possible conjunction of nomadism and flânerie on the frontier of the urban and the edge of gender.

Ulaanbaatar is no Paris. Strolling is not a Mongolian gait. Speed and chaos animate the streets, and the metropolitan foreigner, however practiced in flânerie, stumbles before the onslaught of horses. Multi-horse-powered land-cruisers, that is, the vehicle of choice in this city of nomads. Even the main thoroughfare with traffic lights fails to channel and control the charge of wheels. The dubiously named Enk Taivny Örgön Chölöö, or "Peace Avenue," can be crossed on foot only one lane at a time, as drivers run the lights from all oncoming directions at every chance. With heart-gulping trepidation, I watch from the Avenue's crumbling curb as an elderly woman in a luminous blue *deel* (an embroidered, calflength cloak) launches herself with her cane into the torrent. No one stops as she stumbles between islands of air to the Avenue's opposite bank. When she safely arrives, she kicks up her heels as if pursued by a wolf. How can I, a seasoned flâneuse, affect to follow her? To carry on walking with my usual languor and tactical inconspicuousness is blatantly undoable against this urban tsunami. Mobility is the soul of Mongolia, yet no place on earth so challenges my mobility as does its capital, the "Red Hero." Unheroically, I teeter at the edge of Peace Avenue's commotion and absorb a turbulent rusticity unbecoming to postmodern urbanity. Most world cities, I muse while contemplating my next move, exhibit a fashion-model's cool glamour to lure the "global flâneur." Once the inner city's arch non-conformist, the flâneur now sets the standard for inter-city cruising. A man-about-the-megalopolis, he delights in global travel and he boosts his venture capital by becoming streetwise in emerging market centers, especially those of "developing" nations with novel technologies of urban self-aggrandizement. From Shanghai to Dubai, world cities solicit and display his tasteful cosmopolitanism; their bright lights fail, however, to allure the flâneuse, who lacks the flâneur's expense account and whose peripatetics entails the least expensive savoir faire. Ulaanbaatar, on the other hand, is so far removed from the society of the spectacle that it makes no overtures to the global flâneur. No urban design beckons his speculation. Yet its geopolitical obscurity, together with its rugged eccentricity, appeal precisely to the curiosity of the global flâneuse.

And more than curiosity spurs the flanks of my flânerie. The old woman's bold legwork incites my kinetic reflex to move, if not against the traffic with the flâneuse's characteristic dilatoriness, then astride it with exploratory acceleration. I retreat to the sidewalk and pick up my step, my aimlessness still intact. I feel open to this runaway calamity and oddly unhampered by my appearance, so obviously Western and female with my backpack and hesitant perambulation. As a pedestrian, I pass with readymade invisibility, whereas nothing excites the nomadic gaze so much as the racy SUVs lined up for sale on the few central parking lots. Land cruisers are hot; streetwalkers are not. If "UB," as the natives speed-speak Ulaanbaatar, lacks the commercial seductiveness of world cities, it also lacks the mannequins, models, movie stars, fetish body parts, and other simulacra of commodity femininity. The traffic in mobility trumps the traffic in sex, having driven prostitution off the street to somewhere less horse-powered. Unimpeded by wolf whistles, lewd glances, and opportune groping against which I customarily barricade myself, I let go my lust for pure mobilism. *Yari!* Welcome to the steppe.

Remote yet well connected with the outside world, UB maps an intense crossroads between nomad autonomy and sedentary modernity. I see this directly on the streets before me, in the juncture—or collision—between a billboard advertisement posted by a local furniture-making company ("ANUN") and passers-by who look nothing like the people in the poster. The poster models sit sedately on a surreally elongated sofa, men at one end in suits and hard hats propped against UB's skyline and women at the other in skirts and blouses against some bland domestic interior. Conversely, waves of live men and women roll beneath the billboard with heedless outgoingness, that, together with their traditional and cosmopolitan dress, undermines all that is sedentary and homogeneous. As I start to reckon my global positioning, I see how UB is located midway between metropolitanism and pastoralism, or, more precisely, between urban mobility and "mobile pastoralism" (to borrow a term from Anatoly Khazanov). Less a hustler's city on the make than a nomad's city on the hoof, it has borne a history of unusual movability.

Founded in 1639, as Örgöö, on the site of the Da Khuree monastery, the city moved from place to place until arriving at the present site in 1778. Composed entirely of felt tents, or *gers*, the city could and would be transported to greener pastures when the grass became too dry. When cornerstones were eventually laid, the city became geographically fixed. Yet still, it remains unsettled. Besides the ceaseless and belligerent traffic, there are seasonal migrations of city populations to and from the country, and the unstoppable spread of gers into the surrounding valleys and along the Tuul River. Many of the city's inhabitants do not migrate here to stay but only to winter. Or, they stay long enough to get the training and education that will make them more economically mobile, before they commence with a seasonal relay between their rural homelands and urban careers. Since Mongolia has no privately owned land, newcomers are free to homestead in the city and to tap into its limited and over-taxed infrastructure, namely its coal-fueled electricity and aboveground plumbing. Cities generally facilitate sedentariness, whereas, paradoxically, UB accommodates semi-nomadism. To say the least, it is differently mobile and mobilizes differently than other cities. Even the flâneuse, that most urbane species of human, is moved by its nomadic affects.

Speed, I swiftly discover, affords a semblance of sovereignty for an otherwise unaccommodated pedestrian. But it contradicts the slowness that the flâneuse needs to stake out the city's labyrinthine prospects. Many roads veer off Peace Avenue and great is the chance of getting lost–that is, in both the mundane sense of failing to find one's way and the sublime sense of losing oneself to the city's everyday mysteries. The chances of getting lost in the first sense are increased by the fact that street names are signposted only in Mongolian Cyrillic and well above my literacy level in this language. Add to this the fact that Mongolians get around without addresses that in any case are absurdly minimalist (e.g. "Microdistrict 14, Building 3, Flat 27") and totally meaningless to outsiders like me. Although chances are good for getting lost in the second sense, they increase only with distance from the tourist-trafficked center that entails, simultaneously, increased difficulty in navigating by foot. She who strays beyond Sukhbataar Square and its bordering cafés, bars, discos, boutiques, restaurants, galleries, museums, government and university buildings in search of the Mongolian quotidian, drifts into a bewildering maze of subdistricts and microdistricts, and their archipelagos of gulag apartment blocks and ger encampments. Though I desire to wander through these myriad districts, their residential density and intimacy, as well as the roadless range between them daunt me. Hiring a car or a bicycle is no option, for there are none to rent. Hiring a taxi is an option, but at the cost of self-propulsion. Then again, without enhanced mobility the flâneuse is hobbled on this horse-powered stage. I succumb and hail a taxi, though I am not sure the jeep that pulls over is officially licensed, since in UB every set of wheels is up for hire. Nevertheless, for a set rate of *tögrögs* per mile, my flânerie gains ready passage.

Where to go? I wonder. I can't ask the *jolooch* (the driver) to randomly cruise the neighborhoods. Without speaking Mongolian, how can I explain my desire to flan so that it not be mistaken for blatant voyeurism? Ah, but what's the difference! My next impulse is to follow the crowds to some forum of congregation, where I can mingle and view the urban ordinary askance. This does not mean the tourist crowds that mill about the State Department Store with its compendium of Mongolian mass-produced crafts and souvenirs and its outdoor patio for citywatching over local beer and *buuz* (steamed mutton dumplings). Instead, I tell the driver to take me to the Narantuul Market, which reputedly on windless, summer days like this, assembles mostly Mongolian crowds of as many as 60,000. They come to check out the "black market" in smuggled blue jeans, portable electronics, and "real" vodka as well as seriously practical merchandise. The driver swings onto the perimeter road of Narny Zam and heads towards the Namyanju Street junction. I am saved from a trek along the sidewalkless shoulder where pedestrians are fair game. But we are funneled into a traffic jam short of the market gates. From the jeep, I leap into the mayhem of vehicles, some parked, others idling, and most steering directly into the milieu to pick up or drop off passengers who are keen to avoid more legwork than necessary. Once off and running, the unruly masses career in all directions into a maze of stalls.

Swept into the turbulence, I become a woman of the crowd. I frantically scan the scene for niches of reprieve, but among the infinite kiosks I find no gallery to duck into. Even as I flounder, I can discern that this is not a city farmers' market bringing fresh produce from the country but a hybrid market hawking both urban and rural wear and ware. All around me are racks of men's and women's leather jackets and brightly-colored deels, as well as mounds of baseball caps and traditional Mongolian hats: fur *loovuz*, felt *khongor* hats and silk domed hats–high-brimmed for women, low-brimmed for girls, and spike-topped for men. Once past the jackets and hats, I stumble across the shoes: running shoes, business shoes, high heels and hand-made leather *gutuls*, or riding boots, with curved toes and heels for fitting into (and out of) the stirrup. Gutuls, I learn counter-intuitively, are most popular for promenading the city during Naadam's summer festival, and plastic croc-like slippers are most popular for slopping about outdoors, especially around the animal paddocks. At first, it looks like global gear dominates local fare, but then the circuses of watches, sunglasses, t-shirts, and cameras cannot ultimately compete with the bazaars of riding tack with their variety and abundance of bridles and halters, crops and whips, long-poled *uurga*s (lassos), and, of course, saddles–painted Mongolian, tooled Western—and English dressage saddles as well as basic Russian saddle-like machinations made of rebar and wooden slats.

It is the horse that animates this crowd, I muse, as the equine theme elaborates all around me. Barrels of *airag* (fermented mare's milk) refresh the marketeer at every furlong, while horsehead fiddles (*morin huur*) clamour among the displays of musical instruments. Images of horses appear on CDs, calendars, wallets, placemats, mouse pads, clock faces, and postcards. Surfacing to the top of one postcard pile is a booklet of "art postcards" called "Horse, My Friend." In terms of quantity and variety, top among the hats is the horseback rider's cowboy hat. It would be easy to liken the crowd itself to a herd of horses. Though a herder, not a herd, mentality, seems to steer each nomad on a singular course through the "stockades." A trick, I discover, to navigating this crowd is to become both herd and herder: to go with the stampede and range above it, which my Westerner's extra height allows me to do. Another trick is to project my moving body along a line of flight that curves between other moving bodies, just as the nomads do, thereby avoiding physical contact while keeping apace of the pack. Perhaps, I become a woman of the horde–the Mongol horde of steppe land modernity.

I ride the crowd to the market's edge and wonder why stop here if, already, I am half-way to the country and if it is from the country that Mongolians–even urban Mongolians–derive their sense of the nomadic quotidian? Or, so I guess after glancing through Sharavyn Gerelsaikhan's "photo album," *One Day of Mongolia,* which I find in a market kiosk. Gerelsaikhan's 247 photos compose a series, or montage, of "daily" activities, including protesting, rebelling, rioting, voting, reveling, praying, wrestling, horse racing, horse parading, herding, shearing, tanning, butchering, milking, mining, cooking, dung collecting, dancing, feasting, drinking, marmot trapping, wood chopping, eagle hunting, and ger building and dissembling. Except for protesting, rebelling, and rioting, which are confined to the urban stage, and mining that is now scarifying the mineral-rich, northeastern provinces, all the other activities are essentially pastoral, though many are carried on in the city (wherever gers dominate the landscape). Gerelsaikhan's series alludes to B. Marzan ("Witty") Sharav's famous and eponymous painting, of which a booklet of postcards has been made and that I happen to find next to Gerelsaikhan's "photo album." As I leaf through its facsimile, I see that the painting details hundreds of scenes of country "goings on": it is a bewildering composition (or colorful cacophony?) of nomadic life in all its variety of labor, festivity, and animality across different grassland, desert, and mountain terrains and over changing seasons. Of all these activities, only one would be anachronistic today, namely felt making, which was a prime pastoral activity until the Russians transformed it into a factory industry. Otherwise, the nomadic quotidian that Sharav painted in 1908 still prevails in Gerelsaikhan's 2008 production, as if eighty years of communist modernization has had little effect.

In theory, I could explore most aspects of mobile pastoralism within the nomadic city. But I veto such a plan, remembering not just the difficulty of strolling the ger suburbs but also how UB capitalizes on *One Day of Mongolia* as a tourist gimmick. Even if I were able to outride the downtown traffic, my chances of seeing the nomadic quotidian have already been exploited. I recall Hotel Mongolia's version of *One Day of Mongolia* that it sells to patrons in a packaged "three fold show," complete with a mini Naadam (festival featuring wrestling, archery, and a winning horse prayer song–in place of actual horse racing), a folklore concert (throat singing), and an open-air fire festival (a shaman's dance). I recall, also, eating at the "One Day of Mongolia Restaurant," where I first savored *bansh* and *khuushuur* (boiled and deep fried mutton dumplings), while viewing scenes from Sharav's painting on the restaurant's walls. This tourist replica and regimen does not move me. How could it? If I want to feel the pulse of everyday nomadism and experience mobile pastoralism in its many environments and terrains, then to the country I must go.

I taxi back to Sukhbataar Square, the city's central balcony, from where I can scan the encircling panorama for a way out onto the steppe. Paradoxically, the Square's cement grid offers the pedestrian the only smooth space for ambling with a vista. Here the flâneuse can slow down and look around, taking in the mostly Chinese façades of the surrounding architecture. Bordered by the new Government House to the north, the Central Cultural Palace and State Opera and Ballet to the east, the Mayor's Office to the west, and Peace Avenue to the south, the Square mobilizes public affections that shift mercurially from revelry to revolution to pacifism. (A riot was to break out shortly after I left for the central steppe and only days before Naadam. Supposedly ignited by prodemocracy forces in protest of the recent reelection of the Mongolian People's Revolutionary Party–the old rearguard party that has retained power since the Soviets were deposed in 1991–it resulted in four deaths and numerous injuries). My scanning collides with the statue of Sukhbataar erected in the center of the Square. UB's eponymous Red Hero, Sukhbataar is memorialized for forming alliances with Lenin's Bolsheviks and liberating Mongolia from Manchurian oppression. He is mounted on a horse, which in turn, is mounted on a rock, and his sword is drawn as he commands imaginary legions. But the orbit of my eye sails over him, hailed by the giant, cosmic face of Chingghis Khan engraved into the northern slope of the sacred mountain beyond. The face looks back at the magnificent bronze Chingghis seated at the entrance of Government House, which like every ger opens south towards the sun. From center to periphery my eye travels the imperial arc of Mongolian autonomy. How ironic that this 13th-century warrior-emperor should orient my gaze, and that of every metropolitan Mongolian who looks ahead by looking back to this eternal man of the hour. Since toppling the Soviet regime and installing their own perestroika, Mongolians view Chingghis as their cultural and spiritual leader. His reign over earthly and celestial spheres eclipses Sukhbataar's merely historical fame. Every Nadaam, a ceremonial calvary parades down Surguuli Streeton the Square, bearing the symbolic replicas of the Khan's *sulde*, or spirit banner, made of horsehair from the finest horses and spiriting the city with a spectre of nomadism that once conquered the globe. I hail a jeep and point to the Khan on the mountain. The driver grins and revs.

My first step onto the steppe is, ironically, machine-driven. Yet four-wheeling is fast becoming an acceptable supplement, or even substitute, to four-hoofing. It speeds the transition between urban and pastoral landscapes that now unfolds before me as a passage from dense ger suburbs to *ails* (scattered ger settlements) to the vast steppe where ails of two or three gers sporadically dot the countryside. We cross the Tuul River and head east past women and girls who huddle along the roadside, selling bottled airag, goat hides, sheep heads, and slabs of mutton, as well as livestock for those who like their meat really fresh. We pass the portrait of Chingghis who keenly considers my rural retreat. I am not a passive passenger. The highway transmogrifies quickly into a dirt track that is so rough that my feet bounce off the floorboards, and, to ground myself, I grasp the jeep's handgrip with both hands. As the steppe spreads wider and wider before me, I search creatively for a perspective. In vain. Plateaus encircled by mountains encircle us. The track ahead vanishes through a gap in the nearest range, only to stretch onto the next plateau and through another gap and onto the plateau after that, again and again.

Chingghis disappears from my rear view mirror, as we rock and roll, racing barely ahead of the hurricane of dust raised by our wheels. But then, the metal dome of what looks like a giant helmet looms into the foreground, ascending from the hill beyond the one we now climb. Under the helmet there arises a fierce set of eyes, and beneath these, another set, equally fierce. A man's head. A horse's head. A gargantuan, aluminum Khan, mounted and armed, emerges into full view. I am stunned by not just the suddenness of this apparition but also its colossal incongruity, as if the Panthéon had just erupted onto the plains. Before us: another monumental Chingghis, this time presiding over classical herder terrain. Rising from the middle of nowhere, he is visible from everywhere on this vast steppe.

I marvel at Chingghis's providence. What is the secret to his enduring sovereignty? Long vilified by western Enlightenment history as the barbarian king, against whose hordes the Chinese built their great wall, he has recently enjoyed reappraisal, not only in Mongolia but also around the world, and in popular culture as well as scholarly circles. As I was leaving for Mongolia, two blockbuster movies, Sergei Bodrov's *Mongol: The Untold Story of Ghenghis Khan* and Shinichiro Sawai's *Ghenghis Khan: To the Ends of Earth and Sea* were released in North America. Both movies base their scripts on *The Secret History of the Mongols*, or the story of how Temujin *cum* Chingghis Khan, with heroic perseverance and against all odds, was able to unite Mongolia's warring tribes into a fluid and effective war-machine. The manuscript of *The Secret History* was only recently rediscovered and deciphered, after circulating underground and in code over centuries of Chinese and Russian repression. With the declaration of Mongolian autonomy, Chingghis has been enjoying a national and spiritual resurrection. Abroad, his rising reputation is more puzzling. Though credit for his rehabilitation must go to those international and interdisciplinary teams of scholars who have been busy decoding and translating the manuscript, and producing surprising new interpretations of the Khan's achievements. If they are correct in their reading, we are now to understand that, in addition to warring and conquering, Chingghis introduced the first modern form of globalization and vastly improved the status of Mongol women.

But what the Mongols especially revere about Chinnghis that the outside world has yet to recognize is that the strategies he used to assemble a nation, and later an empire, were progressive *and* nomadic. I sense this from seeing how present nomadic culture thrives alongside economic globalization. Contrarily, the cultural revolution imposed on Mongolia by Russia and China merit no such reverence, or so I detect from the steady dilapidation of Soviet infrastructure and the overt disgust shown for all things Chinese. Lenin and Mao both coerced Mongolia into centralization with methods of collectivization more stratified than Chingghis's processes of unification. Both state totalitarianisms tried to replace nomadic culture with sedentary bureaucracy, and herding with collective farming. Both failed, the Chinese especially, since they leave the degraded grasslands of Inner Mongolia as a telling legacy. No wonder that today's nomads look back to Chingghis, who perfected nomad arts and science, including those of war, to unify the country and conquer the world. Or so I am led to believe by Jack Weatherford's *New York Times* bestseller *Ghenghis Khan: The Making of the Modern World*, which I have brought along as my primary reading. According to Weatherford, Chingghis's mounted battalions covered ground at unfathomable speed, tearing up the boundaries, walls, hierarchies, and hegemonies in their path. In razing feudal fortresses, farms, and cities, they also destratified the land, decentralized states, and opened borders. They mobilized free trade between countries who had never before been in contact, traversing the pan-Asian steppe with caravans of merchants, mathematicians, musicians, linguists, philosophers, architects, engineers, stone masons, metallurgists, and more, back and forth across Inner Asia into the far reaches of Persia, Arabia, China, India, Siberia, and Europa. Transcontinental traffic was set in motion.

Today, Chingghis's comeback aspires to achieve the global presence he assumed in the 13th century, though often in the mundane form of commodity fetishism. His visage is stamped on beer labels, juice cartons, vodka bottles, cigarette packages, company signs and corporate exports. Yet, his is the only face of globalization that emblematizes the survival of nomadism. Before me now, he rises astonishingly high and large against the grassland's infinite horizon. To the Mongols, his name is not Ghenghis, which is a Persian pronunciation, but Chingghis, which in Mongolian means "wolf." He is the Mongols' "wolf totem": an anomaly of pastoralism thriving ferociously in this age of urbanism. It then strikes me: sedentarism not urbanism is the enemy of nomadism.

I decide to trade the jeep for a horse and wander the central steppe within riding range of Karakorum where Chingghis set up his portable capital in 1220. (Permanent structures were erected only after his death in 1226). We re-cross the Khan Kentii Mountains and drive through UB onto the highway leading west out of the city towards the central steppe. The highway quickly downgrades to a dirt road that, in turn, splits into multiple single tracks running beside each other like pack animals.

Tracks across the Steppe. Photograph: Dianne Chisholm.

We drive fast–faster than I can judge which track to select, the jalooch seemingly guided by the smoothest feel under the wheel. Beyond the tracks no further infrastructure remains to be seen. No buildings. No fences. No signposts. Only the odd *ovoo* with its luminous-blue, silk-lined rock-cairns linking earth to sky and invoking Shamanic-Buddhist rites of passage. Nothing corrals the passing of animals, clouds, and Soviet-built vans, indestructible remnants of the former regime.

Ovoo. Photograph: Dianne Chisholm.

Land-cruisers, for all their popularity, never go far outside the city, their mechanism being too complex for trouble-shooting on the steppe, where there are few, if any, garages. Most tour companies supply their main transport vehicle (the dependable Soviet van) with a back-up carrier of extra parts and fuel. From out of nowhere, another jeep and then another catch up to us, and forming a kind of light brigade, we charge three abreast across the steppe. We are surprised by a reverse charge of oncoming vehicles that pass between and around us, including trucks heavily loaded with mounds of raw cashmere, caravans of ger families, followed by stealthily plodding ox-carts hauling all the trappings of a ger ail.

We cross into the big earth and big sky of Arkhangai *aimag* (province) where massive herds of "the five snouts" seem to sprout up spontaneously from the ground. The billowing-bellowing spread of sheep, goats, yaks, and camels, are nothing, however, compared to sweeps of horses, running in herds of up to a thousand head. Mongolia is the only country in the world where horses out-populate humans, as many as thirteen to one. Horses seem to own the landscape. For, as far as I can survey in one steady pan, there are horses in vast numbers—from random herds grazing quietly on the far horizon to crazed, stallion-spurred platoons that trample the steppe at mid-range, to bundles of ditch-water bathers right beside our track. The artsy-horsey landscapes of "Horse, My Friend" acutely mimic this country of horse-love, where horses are given free rein and camels are consigned to heavy-transport duty. In Gerelsaikhan's photo album, all the snouts are featured and always with human handlers, who clearly regard them as a companion species. Only the horse appears in portraiture: at intimate close-range and at aura-enveloped long-range. I've heard it said that a nomad is as worthy as the quantity and quality of her or his animals, horses above all. There are even songs in the nomadic repertoire of *magtaal* (hymns of praise) that are to be sung from the horse's perspective, like the one my driver now sings—the *takhin magtaal*—dedicated to the native horse of the Gobi. I wonder what will happen once my flâneries involve a horse. For never, to my knowledge, has the flâneuse wandered so far from downtown nor by any other means than *au pied*.

By the geothermal springs of Shivert, I exchange my jeep and driver for a horse and herder. With map and charades, I arrange to ride southeast to Karakorum over 120 miles of mixed terrain. The herder, or *malchin*, is a young man of twenty-one. As is customary for steppe nomads, Bagi wears dirt-splattered riding boots and a sky-blue tunic over which he has thrown a coarse, earth-colored deel. The horse, or *mori*, he presents me with is "angry," or so he warns with a malicious frown, and by which he means spirited, as I discover once I take the reins. A pinto gelding, my horse, like all Mongolian horses, has no name but that of his color *khuren alag* (brown and white), which, along with descriptors of temperament and speed, is a primary quality of horseness. Since neither of us can speak the other's language, the malchin and I also go nameless. Curiously, I will soon realize, our namelessness helps me become impersonally attuned to our moving assemblage of human and animal bodies. It also helps to abolish any illusion that I am mistress of my horse.

In a bound, the malchin leaps on his high-pommeled, brightly-painted wooden saddle, while I fumble to launch from the stirrup, a thick circular iron ring best fit for gutuls not flat-soled street-walking shoes like mine. The pinto chews on the bit as if to spit it out, wildly wagging his neck with impatience. The bridle, I note with skepticism, is a ramshackle rawhide affair, and the reins are long, weathered strands that double as a whip or a tether. Whipping is the human part in gait shifting. Mongol horses can be whipped into full gallop from standing still, and into accelerations beyond that. With extra gaits at higher velocities, they are bred to hyperextend themselves over incredible distances. Does this pinto, I dare wonder, descend from the beasts that powered Chingghis' war machine with unrivaled stamina and speed? Here on the steppe, globetrotting construes terrifying meaning.

I am now vaguely mounted. I know and the herder knows that this flâneuse is no horsewoman. So, too, does the horse, and he is testy with my uncertainty. Into the horses's twitching ears, the malchin croons "choo choo," and we take-off at a bolt. We are galloping already yet he whips his bay into faster fury. Swiveling on the saddle and standing upright on the stirrups, he faces me: a grin-grimace smeared above a ruddy brown torpedo. Does he confront me with mockery? No. He wants to race. He whips ever more staunchly, churning horse legs into speed butter. My hands, my knees, the soles of my feet grip reins, mane, pommel, and stirrups in clumsy succession, as my body disassembles in a chaos of contortions. But, whoa: a new coupling of parts repairs my actions and intentions with intuitive mobility. Satisfied, the herder loosens the vise of his gaze and twists his body forward. With our staging grounds far behind and open steppe ahead, flâneuse phenomenology enters a new phase of nomadic mutation. It begins at the core. My body loses unity, but recovers a centre of gravity that feels "not me." In this new assemblage that is part horse, part saddlery, part grasslands, and part sky, "I" am also only a part. Or, to put it another way, "I" am literally, spatially and temporally, beside myself. When *choo choo* escapes my mouth in malchin fashion, it triggers a geo-physiological ballistics. My eyes project from their sockets and land level with the horse's hooves, or snout, in either case stretching my sights along an equine axis. The horse neck torques sideways against the main thrust of the animal's musculature. It throws a signal from the horse brain commanding my focus to become coordinated with the moving horizon. Eyes do. The neck reining stops and a flow of perception begins. The flat indifferent plain promptly morphs into a plane of micro contours and fractal topography. Eye, hoof, and steppe converge in a deft dance of moguls. Unshod, like most Mongol hooves, these hooves tread the grassland with keen proprioception. Detailed arrangements arise under hoof that could never appear under wheel or foot: flowering arcs of diverse grasses, rhizomorphic networks of burrowing mammals, and intricate relays of pasturing herds. Creature populations traverse each other in spreading entanglements: furrowing mice, holey marmots, swarming stubble-grazing insects, circling thermal-riding kites, ger settlements plotted at varying intervals, mountain ranges corralling ever-new convolutions of desert, forest, and plain. At a gallop, the steppe composes a landscape of intertwining mobilities, not all of which are natural or native.

In fact, what opens before me is a meshwork of nomadic pathways and global communications: a frontier of some sort in the making, minus the usual fringe of wilderness. The steppe is open but not wild. Apart from the kites and the occasional eagle's nest, we encounter no wild animals, not even their tracks. I know that in some parts of Mongolia, notably Inner Mongolia, grassland wolves have been hunted to extinction and that the expanding range of domestic herds has forced the withdrawal of the nomadic and ubiquitous gazelle to a reduced territory on the eastern steppe. The grass still grows wild. But no blade is immune from the grazing of a "snout." Then again, this unfenced country strikes me as far from tame. Does it not escape the sedentary grid? Does it not experiment with new ways of becoming mobile and pastoral?

Pastoralism, I observe, is a mix of animal and mechanical mobilities. The many ails we pass on our four-day ride are equipped with land-roving, load-bearing machines. Trucks, jeeps, and vans work alongside camels and bulls to transport *gers*, supplies, and equipment. Parked among the bactrians there is often

Gers, Satellite Discs, and Motorcycle. Photograph: Dianne Chisholm.

a motorcycle. Satellite discs are pitched beside the gers between milk pails and butcher blocks. Throughout the day on our dusk-to-dawn ride, we join a ger family for *tsai* (tea) and *aruul* (curds). Then, I chance to witness a daily orchestration of global distraction and rural labor. During breaks from working–which for men is herding, gelding, branding, killing, and butchering, and for women milking, shearing, cooking, churning, collecting dry dung, stoking the fire, and caring for kids of both kinds–folks tune into satellite TV and a sporadic transmission of various Mongolian, Chinese, Russian, and Japanese programs. In pace with the erratic comings and goings of viewers, there is an anarchic surfing of channels. Best reception more than any personal choice decides what will be watched.

The flâneuse-horse-steppe assemblage in which I take part also experiments with mobility. A "becoming-nomad" of sorts, I am carried outside my accustomed domain with unaccustomed motion. Together, horse, steppe, and woman conjugate speed, distance, horizon. So smoothly we operate, this "angry" horse and I that the malchin starts to test us with more challenging terrain. From open grassland we veer into mountains up ridges lined with larch forests, winding our way through feathery-limbed trees and stirrup-high underbrush. When the forest bogs down, we break for the river and its coulee maze, slip sliding across sandstone cliffs before submerging in water so deep we must swim with our arms around the horses' necks. Then, back onto the grasslands at breakneck speed. For all my meandering across city grids and boundaries, nothing compares with this traversal of ecological zones. Moreover, geo-eco-anatomical mobility entails social mobility. My anonymity does not change, but there is a shift in how I am perceived. To nomad passers-by, as well as to the malchin, I am more than a female foreigner. I am a woman-behorsed. Makeshift and improvised as it is, my horsemanship grants me status. This mobility I enjoy owes nothing to masculinity.

As far as this brief outing shows me, Mongolians of both sexes and all ages are competent riders. If herding is the exclusive occupation of men, excellent horsemanship is expected of everyone. Riding seems to be a great gender leveler, even where traditional gender roles hold sway. Girls, as well as boys, once they see us coming, leap on their horses and gallop out to greet us. Children under ten, including girls, jockey in Nadaam's brutal, multi-day, cross-country horse race. Even little children, who are still just learning the legwork of running across moguls, fling themselves boldly on the back of horse. I will later confirm my observations by watching a number of recent Mongolian films, like *The Story of the Weeping Camel* (2003) and *The Cave of the Yellow Dog* (2005) by Mongolia's internationally-acclaimed female director, Byambasuren Davaa, that use children's animal-borne adventures as a primary vehicle for showing the colorful range of steppe life. In *The Cave of the Yellow Dog* a pre-school age girl, played by a rustic amateur (as Davaa uses nomads to play themselves), goes looking for her runaway dog on a horse four times her size. As she trots out of sight of home territory and into a storm, she is well over her depth. But with confidence in and on her horse, she strikes across the tumultuous landscape until she stumbles upon the ger of a woman shaman and is rescued from exposure. If there is a moral to this passage it might be: "have horse will travel and behold wonders despite dangers."

From a more pragmatic angle, I observe that nomad children ride long distances to attend school at rural community centers. As we say in the West, to be mobile one must be educated. But in Mongolia, the reverse also holds true: to be educated one must be mobile. Put another way, the steppe mobilizes education. How else do I explain that, despite its internal remoteness, Mongolia boasts a 98% literacy rate? Also difficult to explain is the fact that more women than men move to the city to attend university and to become professionals and who are especially adept in foreign languages. Many of the young nomad women I meet on the central steppe indicate that they are here to help their families move the animals to summer pastures before returning to UB to continue with their other careers. Would a girlhood of riding across the grassland prepare Mongolian women with a mobility that extends to the economic sphere? Is their economic mobility not further prepared by a girlhood of seasonal migrations and the interval training this entails in taking down, moving on, and setting up, the rigors of which are mostly conducted by women? I later learn that the reason given for this "reverse" gender ratio in higher education is that men, unlike women, can find good paying country jobs to supplement herding by working with heavy machinery. Hence, parents who wish all of their children to be well employed send their daughters to university in unprecedented numbers. Such reasoning encourages a steppe-land woman to become more flexibly mobile than her brothers. But a nomadic girlhood already prepares her to move on and keep moving in optimally sustainable ways. Having ridden the steppe with its vast horizons before her, how could she not look further afield to the world's larger prospects? Knowing how to move her livestock and livelihood to greener pastures, how is she not best fit to adapt to a globalizing economy and ecology?

Back on the steppe ahead of me, Karakorum emerges into view. We enter town along the Orkhon River, where people are bathing and washing their horses and land-cruisers. The country seems to close in on itself, as we canter past wooden enclosures of gers, huts, and livestock. But it also hooks up routes to myriad points across the country. Dirt tracks converge onto the dusty main road that connects UB in the northeast to Khuijert and Arvaykheer near the Gobi in the south. Lining it on both sides is a jumble of shops, offering basic roadside conveniences: tire shops, tack shops, butcher shops, several restaurants, and saloons selling *airakh* and *airag*. Camel caravans and horse-drawn wagons load up with gear, liquor, and meat, while riders tether their horses at the truck stop, next to vehicles gassing up. The scene strikes me as more "wild west" than Inner Asia, until I see a sandal-shod lama shuffle down the road. He is heading, I expect, to Erdene Zuu Khiid, the country's first and most treasured Buddhist monastery. From midtown, I can make out the turrets of the monastery's fortress. In 1586, Atbai Khan built the monastery next to where Chinnghis Khan's *ger* palace once stood. The more I learn, the more I marvel at the Khans' cosmopolitanism. Accordingly, Karakorum once hosted as many as twelve different religions, while, as the capital of global trade, it hailed merchants from every country that could be connected to it by overland routes. Today, the town still has the feel of a major crossroads, though most traffic arrives from and departs for UB, to where I must presently return. Time to say "bayartai" (farewell) to the malchin and the pinto. I dismount, and with spirited horse legs, I stride over to the truck stop to where I expect to hire a "taxi."

Fourteen hours of driving roughshod later, I am back in UB. Stepping onto Peace Avenue, I find the charge of traffic much less assaulting than when I first arrived. I am to stay at the flat of a friend of a friend before flying home to Canada. Following directions, I find the flat in a typical gulag apartment block not farfrom Sukhbataar Square and next to the State Circus. Sparsely furnished, it is aptly nomadic, though it is not so sparse as to lack a spare room with a writing desk. The flat is rented, I am told, from Elizabeth Chatwin, who, among other things, is the surviving wife of author Bruce Chatwin. Though the former Chatwin is wholly unknown to me, the latter is famous for having invented a free-style form of travel writing and for penning such bestsellers as *Songlines* and *In Patagonia*. He is, perhaps, less famous for proposing to write a popular investigation into "The Nomadic Alternative," that was to explain to himself, and Westerners like him, the cause of his compulsive restlessness. In a letter to his editor at Jonathan Cape, Bruce Chatwin outlined an ambitious book project that he never completed. Instead, he transcribed forty pages of unsynthesized nomadic notations into the narrative text of *Songlines*, thereby executing the intervention that was to become the trademark of his rambling genius. Now that I'm stopping awhile in his wife's Mongolian *pied-a-terre*, I'm compelled to think over what I can remember of "The Nomadic Alternative" with my own nomadic hindsight.

I especially wonder about Chatwin's assertion that nomadism is escapism, an essential, human impulse to flee the metropolitan grid for the defamiliarizing outback. Chatwin was no flâneur: he felt entrapped by the city's domestic regimens and civil routines. Instead, he aligned himself with nomads—literal nomads, that is, like the aborigines with whom he traveled in Australia, as well as literary, classical nomadologists, like Herodotus or Aristeas of Proconnessus, in whose historic footsteps he wrote and walked. By equating nomadism with escapism, Chatwin came precariously close to propounding a naive romanticism. But he complicates the idea with insights into nomadic territoriality. Whether they are hunter-gatherers or herder-pastoralists, nomads are wanderers, who broke out of the forest in pursuit of nomadic and migratory animals. They are also, he recognized, profoundly territorial: they belong to the land and the land belongs to them, though it remains unfenced. Nomads territorialize the land by traversing it repeatedly, and by doing the legwork that is required to know it intimately, as well as by mapping its invisible songlines–its rhizome of animal-geographical-spiritual interconnectivity–in tune with changing landscape ecology. Chatwin may have found in nomadism an "alternative" for all who suffer the urban ennui of modernization. But he did not prescribe the invasion of nomad territory by metropolitan masses in need of mobility therapy. What territoriality, then, becomes the metropolitan Westerner who undertakes the nomadic alternative? How can Chatwin's alternative be "nomadic," if it entails only de-territorialization? How can nomadism be an alternative for urbanites whose "territory" is precisely the city from which she supposedly seeks escape?

I return to the idea of the flâneur–not the heroic flâneur of Balzac's era, when the metropolis was a revolutionary experiment in industrial anthropology, but the defeated flâneur of Baudelaire's era, when revolutionary experiment gave way to commercial expansionism, and the city lost its edge of transition. From the mortifying boredom of bourgeois urbanity, Baudelaire took flight to the city's underworld of public women where he could voyage in sublime evil. He lost his soul but he extended his territory, and he intensified his urban affections. Conversely, Chatwin escaped the city to cultivate his restlessness in the remote elsewhere. Thus, his restlessness characterizes less the nomad than one dispossessed of his lands–a dispossession that, paradoxically, he romanticizes as "nomadic." He did not, to my knowledge ever travel to Mongolia. Had he come here, not to escape but to open the parameters of his metropolitan experience, he would have seen how nomadism and urbanism are not so essentially opposed.

From his vantage as a metropolitan Westerner, which is also my vantage but one I own, Chatwin might have seen that what makes Mongolia so radically different from other "developing" countries is precisely its thriving mix of nomadism and urbanism. He might have seen, even in the post-Stalinist '60s and '70s, that nomadic life in Mongolia is not the exception but the norm. Mongolia bases its autonomy on a sustainable nomadic culture, economy, and ecology that dates at least as far back as Chinnghis Khan. Nomadic territoriality encompasses both city and country, wherever "mobile pastoralism" moves across the land in its various phases of production and distribution. Of a population of two and a half million, one million practice nomadism all year round, while the rest are seasonally nomadic. The steppe belongs to everyone, both women and men, and it is neither publicly nor privately owned. It belongs to nomadic communities who traverse it with their herds, following complex and flexible land-accords between neighboring ails and aimags. True, Mongolia's one big city does little to accommodate the flâneur. But then, flânerie was never supposed to be easy. On the contrary, Ulaanbaatar moves the flâneuse to step well beyond that urban domain to which she has become habituated, and with precisely nomadic mobility. The city's women who straddle the global and the local with adaptive, nomadic fluidity also mobilize her. Flânerie may be fast becoming an anachronism of Western reality (as Baudelaire projected) but here, in Mongolia, nomadism is entering a second era of globalization—this time spearheaded by women.

References

Benjamin, W. (1985). *Charles Baudelaire: A lyric poet in the era of high capitalism.* (H. Zohn, Trans.). London: Verso.

Bilguun. (2008, June). http://asiangypsy.blogspot.com/20008/07/mongoliaelection-2008-updates violence. html.

Bilguun. (2008, June). http://asiangypsy.blogspot.com/2008/07/mongolia-riotsaftermath. html.

Bilguun. (2008, June). http://asiangypsy.blogspot.com/2008/07/mongolian-riotsaftermath-2. html.

Black Horse Ensemble. (2001). *Mongolian traditional.* Ulaanbaatar: RITM Studio.

Bodrov, S. (Director). (2008). *Mongol: The untold story of Ghenghis Khan*. [Motion picture]. Russia: Picture House.

Brosens, P. and Woodworth, J. (Directors). (2008). *Khadak*. [Motion Picture]. Belgium: Bo Films.

Chatwin, B. (1987). *Songlines*. New York: Viking.

Chatwin, B. (1996). The nomadic alternative. In J. Borm and M. Graves (Eds.), *Anatomy of restlessness: selected writings 1969-1989* (pp. 75-106). New York: Viking.

Chisholm, D. (2005). *Queer constellations: Subcultural space in the wake of the city*. Minnesota: University of Minneapolis Press.

Davaa, B. (Director). (2003). *The story of the weeping camel*. [Motion Picture]. Germany and Mongolia: THINKFilm.

Davaa, B. (Director). (2005). *The cave of the yellow dog*. [Motion Picture]. Germany and Mongolia: Tartan Films.

Deleuze, G. and Guattari F. (1987). 1226: The war machine: treatise on nomadology. In *A thousand plateaus* (pp. 351-423). (B. Massumi, Trans.). Minneapolis: University of Minnesota Press.

Gerelsaikhan, S. (2008). *One day of Mongolia: Photo album*. (S. Bayaraa, Trans.). Ulanbataar: Self-published.

Hao, N. (Director). (2008). *Mongolian ping pong*. China: First Run Features.

Humphrey, C. and Sneath D. (1999). *The end of nomadism? Society, state and the environment in inner Asia*. Durham, NC: Duke University Press.

Khazanov, A. M. (1983). *Nomads and the outside world*. (2nd ed.). (J. Crookenden, Trans.). Madison, WI: University of Wisconsin Press. Kohn, M. (2005). Mongolia. Oakland, CA: Lonely Planet.

Lin-Liu, J. (2005, January 31). Mongolia's reverse gender gap. *The Chronicle of Higher Education*.

Rong, J. (2008). *Wolf totem*. (H. Goldblatt, Trans.). New York: Penguin Press.

Sandagdorj, Y. (2008). *Tourist map of Ulaanbaatar*. Ulaanbataar: Map product of Mongolia (MPM©).

Sawai, S. (Director). (2007). *Ghenghis Khan: To the ends of earth and sea*. [Motion Picture]. Japan: Shochiku.

Sharav, B. (2006). *One day of Mongolia*. [Postcard photo reproductions of parts of Sharav's original painting]. Ulanbataar: Gamma Agency and the Zanabazar Museum of Fine Arts.

Tumurtogoo, D. (Ed.). (2007). *The secret history of the Mongols*. (N. Dorjgotov and Z. Erendo, Trans.). Ulaanbataar: Monsudar.

Waugh, L. (2003). *Hearing birds fly: A nomadic year in Mongolia*. London: Acabus.

Weatherford, J. (2004). *Ghenghis Khan and the making of the modern world*. New York: Three Rivers Press.

Walking the Wall:
Global Flâneuse with Local Dilemmas

Kinga Araya

Ringling College of Art and Design

Abstract

In the essay I will critically introduce and discuss some of my key "walking" performance artworks that emphasize the phenomenon of walking and talking in-between different countries, cultures and languages. More specifically, since my infamous walking away from Poland, while on a student trip in Florence, Italy in 1988, I have been trying to exercise my freedom of movement and speech while living in Italy, Canada, Germany, and currently, in the USA. The desire to make artworks that would express some of the walking ideas was very important to me.

Introduction: Traveling Identity

It is quite special for me to write about global flânerie while reflecting on two distinct events: a physical act of unpacking in my new place and an extended celebration of my personal and artistic staggering from the Eastern to the Western World. The first special circumstance presents a deceivably simple and mundane act of unpacking my belongings in a rental house in Sarasota, Florida, where I moved on August 15, 2009. After leaving Montreal in September 2006 and having worked and traveled as a post-doctoral fellow in Philadelphia and Berlin, I realized that this is my thirteenth "home" since I left Canada. Living with and from suitcases has already become my specialty since I defected Poland during the summer of 1988, simply walking away from a student trip in Florence, Italy. At that time, I was not able to critically reflect on my new emerging identity as it was inserting itself into an international and global economy. I was simply too close to my own immigrant experience, coping primarily with the questions of survival: "What and when am I going to eat? Where am I going to sleep?" These questions underscored a political and economic schism that I was feeling right in my body, the body that needed food and rest, and simultaneously, the body perceived as a cast-off subject, an abject thrown into the promising Western World. Italy offered different living and legal situations controlled by diverse rules that were all new to me, a person born and brought up "behind the iron curtain." During the immigration time, I was learning how to be patient when facing numerous cultural and political challenges while negotiating my Eastern-European identity, flavored by my parents' exilic history. My mother was born into a Tartar-Muslim family in Vilnus; my father was a child of Polish parents who adopted Ukraine as their homeland. Yet in 1939, because of the consequential historical moment, their families were exiled from their homes to find themselves estranged and terrified in Nazi-occupied Poland. Perhaps my state of exile was always already inscribed in the history of my family and somehow helped me to face the challenges of globalization.

Interestingly, even though my walking away from a student trip happened in Florence, I never had the pleasure to enjoy walking around this enchanting Renaissance city. My short promenade led from the Baptistery, (where I intensely prayed while making a decision of walking away from Poland), to a house of a young Italian actress whom I met during an alternative Gardzienice Theatre Workshop in Poland the summer before. I still wonder how we managed to communicate since at that time I spoke only Polish and my Florentine friend (I believe her name was Francesca) spoke only Italian. I was keeping a scrupulous diary during the entire trip, and the notebook became one of the most precious items that traveled with my humble belongings to Canada. During one of the multiple apartment moves, I lost this priceless diary that now would answer many of my questions regarding that remarkable summer of 1988.

As I unpack my numerous boxes, crates, pieces of luggage, suitcases and bags (most of which were not opened since August 2006), the fragmented notes, faded photos, and broken objects fall out unexpectedly, piercing me with their potent and layered history. All these items belong to me, although many ended up in my possession while traveling in mysterious and rhizomatic ways throughout the East and West-Africa, North America, Middle East and Asia. All those objects "throw me out of balance" and slow down my actual unpacking. The sharp division between global and local emerges as I unwrap an African mask, cast glass boomerangs, undeveloped film negatives, and letters guaranteeing love beyond any national and cultural borders, declaring passionate promises now as faded as the lover's words on the page. This is not a simple act of moving into a new place. This is the thirteenth test (taking only *the last three years* into consideration) to find my own place and space. I believe that the global flâneuse is supposed to face and accept all sorts of difficulties and challenges. Shall I accept this layered personal, artistic and professional moving around the world in high hopes of reconciling my dwelling within and beyond the shifting abodes?

The second distinct event that still resonates within me refers to the twenty-year anniversary of defecting from Poland while in Italy. My recent art exhibition in Berlin entitled *Ten Steps* commemorates the event in video, photo and audio artworks. What was particularly special for me was the fact that my summer exhibition was in the former Border Watchtower—Grenzwachturm Schlesischer Busch—now transformed into an art gallery. This tall and narrow building, with impossibly vertical stairs up to the second floor, once stood right at the border of East and West Berlin. Its history refers to a peculiar non-place, and it was indeed the most appropriate building to house my itinerary artworks. The exact twenty-year anniversary of walking away from Poland was in 2008 when I was in Berlin and decided to walk along the ruins of the Berlin Wall for ten consecutive days with actual and virtual walkers. It became my longest and most engaging walking artwork to date, and its personal and theoretical multilingual discussions on walking and exilic experiences accompanied by art, documents, and objects, emphasizes the global and local tensions. The video documentation's introductory narration is accompanied by the wobbling images of me walking around the former Refugee Camp in Rome, taken in the summer of 2008. Its suggestive narrative sets the context of the *Walking the Wall* performance and the present discussion of global flânerie.

Former Border Watchtower, Berlin, German. Photograph: Kinga Araya.

recent art exhibition in Berlin entitled *Ten Steps* commemorates the event in video, photo and audio artworks. What was particularly special for me was the fact that my summer exhibition was in the former Border Watchtower—Grenzwachturm Schlesischer Busch—now transformed into an art gallery. This tall and narrow building, with impossibly vertical stairs up to the second floor, once stood right at the border of East and West Berlin. Its history refers to a peculiar non-place, and it was indeed the most appropriate building to house my itinerary artworks. The exact twenty-year anniversary of walking away from Poland was in 2008 when I was in Berlin and decided to walk along the ruins of the Berlin Wall for ten consecutive days with actual and virtual walkers. It became my longest and most engaging walking artwork to date, and its personal and theoretical multilingual discussions on walking and exilic experiences accompanied by art, documents, and objects, emphasizes the global and local tensions. The video documentation's introductory narration is accompanied by the wobbling images of me walking around the former Refugee Camp in Rome, taken in the summer of 2008. Its suggestive narrative sets the context of the *Walking the Wall* performance and our discussion on global flânerie.

Due to extraordinary personal circumstances and my anti-Communist activities, I was not allowed to travel abroad. Upon a special request and a personal written guarantee that I would return to Poland, the local police authorities granted me my passport and I obtained a tourist visa. I was ready for my first student trip to Italy. Once in Florence, against all odds and restrictions imposed upon me, I decided to exercise my freedom and simply walked away from our bus. I left everything behind. Somehow I knew that I would not be given another chance. This was my time. The next day I hitchhiked to Rome, where I joined a group of young, Polish immigrants living in a tall building behind Largo di Boccea, now the ruins of a once supervised and overpopulated refugee camp. It was during my Italian immigration that I composed my first short poems, entitled *Dziesiec Krokow* (Ten Steps). At that time I had no idea that I was already dealing with my two artistic tropes, walking and talking, which have been accompanying me on my creative journeys.

Krok pierwszy

Nie mam pojecia jak sie pisze A
Z jedna krzywa nozka czy dwiema
B jest jeszcze trudniejsze
(to kilkugodzinne studium w ciemnych skryptoriach labiryntu sredniowiecznego)
Ty zas mowisz
Ze alfabet nie istnieje
Wymysl diabla spod litery
Z (Araya, 1989)

(My free translation):

First Step

I have no idea how to write A
With one crocket leg or two
B is even more difficult
(it is a time consuming studium in the dark scriptoria of medieval labyrinths)

And you say that alphabet does not exist
That it is a devilish trickery under the letter
Z

    I remember how anxious I was upon returning to Europe in 2007. I was wondering how I could honor this special time that marked the twenty-year anniversary of my walking away from Poland. Initially, I did not plan to walk 160 km along the site of the Berlin Wall, yet it turned out to be the signature work of my post-doctoral fellowship at the ICI Institute for Cultural Inquiry in Berlin, Germany. After executing my 2008 walking performance in Berlin, I experienced a strange case of iconoclasm towards my own images. What was I afraid of? And did the act of walking affect this iconoclasm in some way and if so, how? I believe that the physical impossibility of walking in Sarasota, Florida, the activity that I truly cherish, was one of the major reasons of my unexpected iconoclasm that shocked me to my bones. I will come back to the challenges of

Performing Exile: Walking the Wall, **2008. Photograph: Kinga Araya.**

performance in Berlin, walking in this typically "car city" later on in this essay. My walk along the former Berlin Wall was not a predictable performance artwork. It was filled with intense logos and pathos. It was about meditating on my slow transformation from an Eastern European subject, who wanted to assert herself as a freestanding and creative subject in the West. It was about falling down and getting up because of my political, linguistic, and cultural unfitness within Italian and Canadian laws concerning immigration and citizenship. It was about the unmeasurable weight of living twenty years in the shadow of the iron curtain and twenty years in the West. (Araya, 2009).

Etymology of the Words Flâneur and
Flâneuse and their Cultural Contexts

In order to contextualize my walking and talking artworks within global flânerie, it is important to refer to the etymology of the word *flâneur* and its gendered counterpart, *flâneuse*. In her informative essay, "The Invisible Flâneur," Elizabeth Wilson presents a feminist critique of gendered modernist spaces, examining the phenomenon of the flâneur in the context of the empowered male figure, while the female stroller, the flâneuse, is presented as a powerless walker not only in modern, but also in postmodern public spaces. Wilson provides a useful etymology of the word *flâneur*. The fact that the origins of the word are uncertain yet the first dictionary definitions support the gendered meaning of flâneur is critical for Wilson. She note that the 19th-century *Larousse Encyclopaedia* already had two gendered entries: flâneur and flâneuse. The latter denotes "a kind of reclining chair . . . it looks like an extended deck chair, and welcomes its occupant with womanly passivity" (Wilson, 1996, p.76). Wilson's feminist reading of the 19th-century origins and social functions of the flâneur make her examine the identity of the modern stroller as a typically masculine activity of "loitering, frittering away of time" (Wilson, 1996, p. 62). The flâneur presents as the male figure in the Parisian metropolis whose favorite activities consist of disinterested walking around Paris and observing the urban marvels and the crowd. Wilson follows a historical development of the term *flâneur* by examining its earliest literary uses in the novels by Balzac, Zola, Proust, and Dickens in which the male city strollers play the main literary characters. Further, she examines in greater depth an anonymous French pamphlet from 1806 that introduces the figure of the flâneur in the context of Bonaparte's era. A passage from the pamphlet, *Le Flâneur au salon ou M.Bon-Homme: Examin joyeux des tableaux, mele de vaudevilles*, exhibits some of the key characteristics of the flâneur that will become critical in the later creative and critical writings about the strolling urban figure by Baudelaire and Benjamin:

> No one knows how M. Bonhomme [the flâneur] supports himself, but he is said to be a rentier, seemingly set free from familial, landowning or mercantile responsibilities, to roam Paris at will. The flâneur spends most of his day simply looking at the urban spectacle; he observes in particular new inventions: for example he stops in Place Louis XIV to examine the signals of the marine telegraph, although he understands nothing about them. (Wilson, 1996, p. 62)

Wilson explains that M. Bonhomme engages in aesthetic activities because either he was an artist or he associated himself with the artists in the modern public spaces of the salons, boulevards, arcades, cafes, bars, theaters and brothels. M. Bonhomme, however, seems to perform a marginal flânerie. He is a solitary stroller with a blasé attitude towards the modern city.

When we compare the most recent dictionary entries of the word *flâneur*, we find striking similarities with the 19th-century *Larousse* definitions of the same French word. Along with the literary quotations of the literary uses of *flâneur*, the eighth volume of *Tresor de la langue Francaise-Dictionaire de la langue du XIX et du XXe siècles* offers two main definitions of the word that describe walking in the city as a rather disinterested, care-free strolling about town. More specifically, *flâner*, as a transitive verb, is first defined as "avancer lentement et sans direction précise," and the second meaning denotes "perdre son temps; se complaire dans l'inaction, dans le farniente" (p. 953). Further, under the entry *flâneuse* there is a simple explanation of "celui, celle, ce qui flâne", as well as the definition of *flâneuse* as a "long chair" already quoted by Wilson: "siege pliant en bois ou en osier pouvant faire office de chaise longue" (p. 953). The latter definition of *flâneuse* as "chaise longue" does not come from the 19th-century entry; it is quoted after Sandry-Carr's publication in 1963. By comparison, the *Oxford English Dictionary* from 1989 has a much shorter entry of the word *flâneur*, and the definition of *flâneuse* does not appear at all. The noun *flânerie* is defined as "the disposition or practice of an idler or lounger", and *flâneur* as "a lounger or saunterer, an idle man about town" (p. 1003).

The flâneur presents a new performing identity that was born in rapidly changing mid-19th century Paris restructured by Baron Georges Haussmann. As a chief administrator in Paris, appointed by the Napoleon III, Haussmann not only widened the existing streets of Paris and built twenty-two new boulevards, but also modernized the whole city plan, producing great traffic arteries, the sewer system, and the impressive construction for the *Exposition Universelle* of 1867. The 19th-century architectural transformations were made at a high cost by destroying most of old Paris and its living social structures. While on one hand, Paris proudly showed off its enhanced architecture, streets, and boulevards, on the other hand, a growing number of homeless (qua: walkers), dispossessed people were pushed away from the cleaned-up, public spaces of the modern city that started to become an estranged space for its own inhabitants.

Charles Baudelaire gave us not only an account on what constitutes modernity, but also the characteristics of the modern hero. In "The Painter of Modern Life," Baudelaire introduces a figure of the flâneur exemplified by the artistic endeavor of a genius. He defines him in the following way:

> observer, philosopher, flâneur—call him what you will; but whatever words
> you use in trying to define this kind of artist, you will certainly be led to
> bestow upon him some adjective which you could not apply to the painter
> of eternal, or at least more lasting things, of heroic or religious subjects.
> (Baudelaire, 1964, p. 4)

The modern painter, then, is concerned with both eternal and fugitive beauty. He is an empowered "man of the crowd," a "great traveler and cosmopolitan" who observes life unfolding around him with the curiosity of a child. The flâneur's activities of examining Parisian life while moving through the city support the discourses of power of the 19th-century society of the spectacle. The question of who could visually scrutinize the modern world became an important socio-political issue. Baudelaire's flâneur, a "prince who everywhere rejoices in his incognito" (Benjamin, 1999, p. 9), represents a privileged figure of 19th-century public life because he can define space by his anonymous and carefree mobility through the city. Nevertheless, a flâneur has no real social or political power. In his persistent homeless walks, he spies in and out of the urban frame and keeps moving. Benjamin states that, "it takes a heroic constitution to live through modernism" (p. 74). The German critic also refers to Jules Laforgue's text about Baudelaire, quoting that he was the first to speak "as someone condemned" to live in Paris (Benjamin, 1999, p. 55). Baudelaire describes the characteristics of a dispossessed flâneur and a modern hero in a decadent way, wearing "the black suit and the frock" (Benjamin, 1999, p. 77). A modern hero then, a socially powerless artistic figure, an intellectual, is dressed in black as if he were mourning something essential and disappearing from his life: the very originality and liveliness of modernity. It is critical that it is by the means of walking, the most humble human experience, that the city stroller becomes aware of the "fragility of modern existence" (Benjamin, 1999, p. 77).

In his critical analysis of the Baudelairean modern world, Benjamin scrutinizes the experience of the flâneur as a discontinuous and rhapsodic performance. He examines several figures that complement the figure of the flâneur, exemplified in the Baudelairean literary heroes of the apache, the dandy, the detective, the conspirator and of such social outcasts as the prostitute and the ragpicker (the homeless person). Out of the six flâneurs' alter egos there is only one female character, a prostitute, in French called *peripateticienne*, the one who walks the city. The Parisian world of the *demimonde* presents one of the most complex features of socio-historically understood modernity. From Baudelaire and Benjamin, we learn that modernity in the last exhaustive years of the *fin de siècle* was obsessed with the female body. In numerous theoretical discourses as well as in the artistic and literary representations, the female nude was very desirable to the ruling white, heterosexual bourgeois class. In assuring the pleasure of looking—*scopophilia*—the bourgeoisie had not only to be surrounded by prostitutes and their images, but also had to have the power of controlling the situation. In a detailed study of Manet's painting of a well-known Parisian prostitute, *Olympia*, for example, T. J. Clark refers to the social and controlled "necessity" of making the prostitutes circulate throughout the modern city (Clark, 1984, p.103). In a complex, sexually charged socio-historical discourse, a prostitute became one of the dispossessed walking symbols of the commercialized and commodified modern city.

Both Baudelaire and Benjamin knew that the development of the modern metropolis was paid for dearly with the massive commercialization of every possible product. The limits of modern transactions were set as high as the sale of Paris's own inhabitants. This situation is exemplified by the growing business of buying and selling the services of the prostitute-peripateticienne. She was becoming a desirable and salable modern object, and she had to remain "an invisible flâneur." However, Baudelaire glorifies the prostitute as the muse of the modern poet in many of his poems. He writes, "holy prostitution of the sound which gives itself wholly, poetry and charity, to the unexpected that appears, to the unknown that passes" (Baudelaire, 1964, p. 56). Other so-called fallen women, or women "in revolt against society" (Baudelaire, 1964, p. 37), such as lesbian, single, and independent women, became a source of fascination for Baudelaire. Exalted by her imagined mythical power and freedom, Baudelaire writes that the "lesbian is the heroine of modernism because she combines with a historical ideal the greatness of the ancient world" (Baudelaire, 1964, p. 90).

There is an important transition for some unemployed and marginal Parisian walkers who become part of the new bourgeoisie. Benjamin quotes Rattier's utopic novel from 1857 entitled *Paris n'existe plus* that describes the modern city as a place where making rapid social changes in the city dwellers is possible, because of the rapid economic and political modifications happening in the metropolis. In particular, Rattier says:

> The flâneur who we used to encounter on the sidewalks and in front of the shop-windows, this nonentity, this constant rubberneck, this inconsequential type who was always in search of cheap emotions and knew about nothing but cobblestones, fiacres, and gas lanterns has now become a farmer, a vintner, a linen manufacturer, a sugar refiner, and a steel magnate (Benjamin, 1973, p. 54).

Analyzing one of Baudelaire's poems from *Les Fleurs du mal*, Benjamin interprets the Parisian crowd as anonymous and detached, but also as inspirational for the poet-flâneur. There is a serious preoccupation with the paradoxical entrapment of the flâneur in the metropolitan transient sites that produced him and with the same sites that also started to erase the flâneur's individuality. Benjamin calls a modern flâneur an accomplice who takes part in the overpowering urban spectacle. The phenomenon of the modern city acquires the quality of what defies human physical and psychical limits. In other words, the city becomes an artistic locality where individuals have strong aesthetic feelings. In that powerful sublime spectacle, however, the identity of the modern flâneur seems to be threatened by the very fact that he is one among many. Benjamin argues that the modern stroller finally acquires a commodity value that renders him grotesque. In critically summarizing Baudelaire's writing on the modern hero and his alter egos, Benjamin observes that the "flâneur, apache, dandy and ragpicker were so many roles to him [the flâneur]. For the modern hero is no hero, he acts hero. Heroic modernism turns out to be a tragedy in which the hero's part is available" (Benjamin, 1973, p. 97).

Flânerie: From Local to Global to Local

There are at least two critical aspects regarding the dialectics of global and local flânerie. They are often present in my artworks that dialogue with the phenomenon of walking and talking in between countries, cultures and languages. First of all, since globalization maps the world unevenly, it often stands in opposition to local and individual experiences. The fact that uneven distribution of economy created different types of "worlds" is not a surprise. The thicks and thins of global economy made many citizens exiles in their own countries. Since many of them cannot participate in the mainstream politics and economy, they are forced to live and work in a place determined by larger power structures. They are people who can hardly relocate, travel, and work as they would prefer. Their localities, therefore, become the only world they know. There are many cultural examples of breaking away from the "local politics," often run by oppressive and totalitarian governments. Some of the great artists, who under diverse yet never easy circumstances, made an extraordinary transition from East to West, became critical cultural advocates for local and global worlds. Such artists who immediately come to my mind are Vera Frenkel, Ewa Partum, Marina Abramovic, Krzysztof Wodiczko, Jana Sterbak, and Christof Javacheff, amongst others. Their examples tell us that in order to become "global" one has to lift oneself above the "local" experience, even though the "local" remains a critical element that defines who the individual is and what itinerary he/she undertook to function in the West.

My argument is that the two positions, the global and the local, are still not reconciled because we are constantly reminded of our wanted or unwanted "locality," depending on the global situations. We do participate in a complex socio-political and cultural economy that divides East from West, the provincial city from the metropolis, and the first—from the third-world. I would like to quote two poignant examples of one's global unfitness within local contexts. One of them is from my conversation with Polish feminist and conceptual artist Ewa Partum in her Berlin apartment. While we were talking about the situation of women artists in the East and West, Partum told me that some of the Western curators claim that her artworks cannot be sold for the same price as other conceptual artists' works from the West because she is from the "East block." This "localizing statement" is particularly disturbing because Partum has been living in Berlin for over thirty years and has been producing significant bodies of work in the West.

The second example refers to my experiences of daily walks on North Tamiami Trail in Sarasota, right in the college neighborhood where I teach. I was told that this area is known for its working street girls, apparently a prime pick-up and drop-off for the prostitutes. Since I do not have a driver's license, I can rely only on my two legs and a limited Sarasota public transportation. In other words, I have to walk about 15 minutes to get to school, and if I want to go downtown I can catch a bus or walk about forty minutes. I must confess that this is the first time in my life that I experience walking at its absolute limits. Every single time I make my necessary walks on North

Tamiami Trail, I hear derogatory and sexist remarks from most of the male walkers, men on bikes, and some drivers who honk, slow down and look curiously at me. I do not provoke these men in any way, and yet they disturb my daily walks to and from work. My initial shock of finding myself in a public sphere that is so oppressive has helped me to understand how the 19th-century flâneuse might have felt when she was discouraged to walk alone in public spaces because they would be taken for *peripateticienne*. In such a difficult context where every walk on Tamiami Trail is read in a local discriminatory language, I wonder how much work one has to do to reach the global context. My walking on Tamiami Trail became such an unbearable personal experience that I decided to turn it into yet another performance artwork, *Walking Tamiami Trail* to be executed in the near future. In particular, I will be walking the urban part of a very long Tamiami Trail street (that joins Tampa in the North and Miami in the South). Some of the challenges of the socio-cultural limits of walking in Sarasota will be documented in video, audio and photography.

My most recent performance, *Walking the Wall*, and the subsequent video are also good examples of exposing this dialectic tension of local versus global. On the one hand, I was not allowed to travel abroad and was grounded to stay "at home;" on the other, I defied the absurdities of the Communist restrictions and simply walked away. Some of those artistic examples show us that the local plays an important, if not a critical role, in understanding the global.

Performing Walking and Talking

For me putting one foot in front of the other was never about becoming a global flâneur or a flâneuse, it was about survival. The compulsion of walking towards the West was filled with a mythic desire that "life is elsewhere," and I did not look back at the ruins of the Iron Curtain, a burden engraved in the silenced and humiliated faces of Polish citizens. I thought that my defection in Florence, Italy announced a pilgrimage towards the Promised Land; instead, I began my personal art of fugue that introduced many harmonic steps and transitions, all played intensely without breaks and stopping points. I was reminded too many times that I was from the East, from Poland; therefore I was not fully autonomous and empowered as a subject. I never understood why this would have to be emphasized so many times, why the "local" has to be brought up when the "global" is supposed to go beyond the racial and national differentiation. Interestingly enough, my Eastern-European background was only an "issue" when the decisions about obtaining a job, entering certain scholarship and fellowship competitions, and freedom to travel presented themselves. However, once I obtained Canadian citizen status, the logistics of travel changed for me. Suddenly, travel became less humiliating, and I was passing the Western checkpoints much faster and without lengthy questions. When I opened my mouth, however, it was clear that English is not my first language, and things were getting complicated with procuring employment in Canada. One of my early videos entitled *ABC*, comments on that uneven global-local dialectics where even the judge, an official representative of the Canadian Law, acts in a discriminatory manner towards the immigrants. The narration of the story "B as in BULLSHIT," is recited very slowly. It goes as follows:

> In November of 1993 I had a special interview with a citizenship judge at the court of Canadian Citizenship in Ottawa. The oral interview regarding Canadian geography, history and politics was a condition *sine qua non* to obtain a Canadian citizenship status. The middle-aged woman judge dressed formally in a gown, greeted me and asked me to sit down. The interview started. The judge looked straight into my eye, protruded her face towards me and making exaggerated staccato pronunciation of every single word asked me: "Who—is—the—prime—minister—of—C-a-n-a-d-a?" (Araya, 1997).

My second premise is that those unpresentable, unspeakable, and yet unique "local" experiences are very valuable and they show us that there is much more to the image of the dominant and happy "global narrative." The tension between global and local lies in many great contemporary artworks that often take political and conceptual critique of the cultural *status quo*. Some of my artwork that address those issues more directly are *Peripatetic and Orthoepic Exercises*; *Walking Around*; *Octopus*; *Grounded (I), (II); and (III)*; *PolCan, Walking with Arms*;

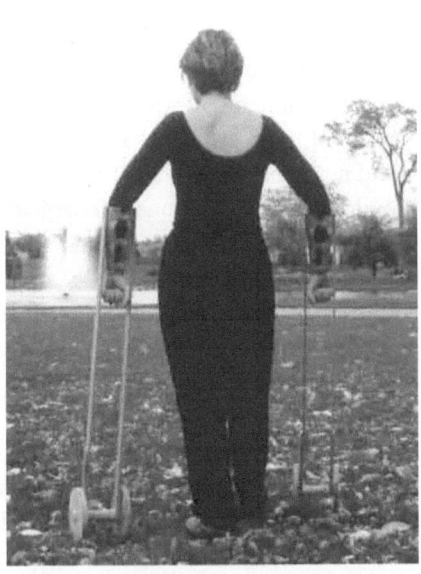

***Walking with Arms*, 2002. Photograph: Kinga Araya.**

Exercising with Princess Headgear (Adjustable); and *Fifty-Five*. One of my earliest sculptural performances from 1998, entitled *Peripatetic Exercise*, challenges the notion of walking while wearing heavy shoes: two cast iron hemispheres with imprints of my feet in the middle of each. In spite of the difficulty of balancing in the shoes, I attempt at the same time to play the Vivaldi *Concerto in A-minor* (a piece I learned as a child). During *Orthoepic Exercise*, I walk around a swivel pole with a two-meter long extension of my tongue inserted into my mouth. My beautifully threatening instrument for correct (ortho) speech (orthoepy) sets up conditions for the war of pronouncing the words rightly. For this piece I performed in the enclosed and unifying space of a soundproof studio. It was a non-place, where the emerging language of violin and metal met as I walked around the swivel pole followed by the squeaky sound of an iron tongue weighing twenty-four kilograms. *Exercising with Princess Headgear (Adjustable)* was performed in a public space as I was climbing Mount Royal in Montréal. Dressed in black, I wore a beautiful yet cumbersome and dangerous copper hat that weighed about ten kilograms. *Walking with Arms* was the fourth interpretation of my walking and took place in each of the four seasons in Montréal's Jarry Park. In this case the prostheses are made out of maple wood and leather. These paradoxical extensions of the arms do not facilitate bodily movement. On the contrary, they represent grotesque attachments that exemplify the very impossibility of undertaking any unrestrained journey through time and space. The four "walking" artworks refer to the notion of prosthetics and they open up areas of indeterminacy that speak not only about aesthetics and beauty, but also about power relations. They problematize a formation of the self that has always been inscribed within the most immediate local context of family and community, extending towards the larger context of national and global dilemmas. The only two performances that were both tested in Poland and Canada were *Grounded (I)* and *(II)*, performed with the third prosthetic leg, and *PolCan*, wobbling and falling down because of the impossible red and white shoes, walking to the slowed-down cadence of the Polish and Canadian national anthems. It was interesting for me to experience the development and the reception of these art pieces in my homeland and in my adopted country, Canada. While I did not experience major differences in the execution of the pieces, performing in Poland was more emotionally charged and more people (along with the media) were interested in my personal and artistic reasons for "coming home" to perform. Those two performances shared in the local and global dialectics and helped me to connect two of my distinct experiences, Polish and Canadian.

Coda

My personal, artistic and intellectual displacements that took me from Europe to North America and made me walk between music, theatre, art history, comparative literature, and visual arts. I realized that I perform at my best while engaging in a variety of artistic practices ranging from drawing, painting, photography, video, sound, sculpture to performance and installation art. Most of my artworks produced since

1996 address the reclamation of the body through differing and deferring discourses on loss. Often arranged in an installation situation, my art engages in the discourse of power relations where the rights of free speech and unrestrained movement through space are put into question.

My theoretical and visual research performed in Poland, Italy, Canada, Germany and United States, welcomes a variety of intellectual contributions that have been teaching me how to walk and talk responsibly, how to make culture in a different way. The theories that served as important source of inspiration for me, such as the deconstructive philosophy of Jacques Derrida and the psychoanalytical and critical examinations of the estranged and exilic "self" by Julia Kristeva and Edward Said, remain important parts of making art and doing academic research. In a certain way, they already announced and participated in the dialectics of the global and the local. Writing from different academic perspectives, Derrida, Kristeva and Said forcefully argue that a stranger, an exile, a cast-off subject, puts cultural politics into crisis because she performs in opposition to institutionalized and globalized culture. I believe that speaking from an interdisciplinary space composed of personal and universal stories offers a great possibility to challenge ourselves and ask more critically, who we are and why we are where we are. By insisting on building walking and talking prostheses in iron, glass, copper and wood, and on walking the Berlin Wall, I aspire to seize the meaning of the self where the dichotomy of personal and universal does not exist. Constantly performing as an estranged body that moves in and out of socio-political and cultural frames, I deliberately exercise my artistic language by trying to transgress local and global worlds and to make sense of our personal and artistic flânerie in the world that both promises and denies.

References

Araya, Kinga, *Dziesiec krokow* (*Ten Steps*), 1989. Araya, Kinga, *Ten Steps*, video, 2009. Araya, Kinga, *ABC*, video, 1998.

Baudelaire, Charles. (1964). *The painter of modern life*. (Jonathan Mayne, Trans.). London: Phaidon Press.

Benjamin, Walter. (1968). "On some motifs in Baudelaire." In *Illuminations. essays and reflections*. (Hannah Arendt, Trans.). (pp. 155-200). New York: Shocken Books.

Benjamin, Walter. (1973). *Charles Baudelaire: A lyric poet in the era of high capitalism*. (Harry Zohn, Trans.). London: NLB.

Benjamin, Walter. (1997). "Paris, capital of the nineteenth century." In Neil Leach (Ed.), *Rethinking architecture: A reader in cultural theory* (pp. 33-40). New York: Routledge.

Benjamin, Walter. (1999). *Walter Benjamin: Selected writings, vol. 2, 1927-1934* (Rodney Livingstone, Trans.). Cambridge, Massachusetts: The Belknap Press of Harvard University Press.

Clark, Timothy. (1984). *The painting of modern life: Paris and the art of Manet and his followers*. New York: Knopf.

Watson, Sophia & Gibson, Katherine. (Eds.). (1996). *Postmodern cities and spaces*. Oxford, United Kingdom: Blackwell.

Kyoto blog: 87 Days in Kyoto

Lori Ellis

State University of New York Cortland

Abstract

In February, the streets are quiet. Buses are silent. Only eyes are revealed beneath hats and scarves, and yet I feel welcomed. I am bowed into and out of restaurants, stores, temples, galleries, and gardens. Within these orderly frames there are constant delights for the eye, ear, nose and palate. I am seduced and consumed by the sensual. By May, I have fallen into and out of love with every quarter of the city many times over. The forces and rhythms that affect my developing relationship with Kyoto are recorded by the almost daily entries of the Kyoto blog.

Braille Sidewalks
Saturday, February 7, 2009

I've been walking Kyoto's streets all day and into the night for five days now. There have been so many new sights, rhythms and sensations that many are still jumbled, waiting to fall into place and fully into consciousness. At this point my feet are also a bit tender so I began to feel every small bump and crevice in the sidewalk's surface. I began to sense repetition and groupings and realized that I was walking over sets of round bumps and sets of lines like Morse code. The line sets moved straight forward, usually in the middle of the sidewalk and then met the sets of circles just before crossings or when changing directions.

The dawning finally came when my hand hit a bit of braille on a handrail as I followed a path down into the subway station and found that the paths led to subway maps with braille-raised surfaces. Still not trusting myself I was not convinced of my interpretation until this morning when I saw a sight impaired citizen using the system. Fabulous! Has anyone ever seen this in another city?

Braille Sidewalks, 2009. Photograph: Lori Ellis.

Torii gates
Monday, February 9, 2009

One can hardly walk in Kyoto for five minutes without seeing the torii gate of a Shinto shrine. There are reportedly 40,000 Shinto shrines in the city. Large, small, intermingled in neighborhoods, shopping arcades, or on grand real estate on the sides of mountains.

Fushimi Inari Shrine (founded in 711) occupies the whole of Mount Inari and holds one thousand torii gates for pilgrims to pass through. To walk up the mountain and return through all one thousand gates took us close to four hours. This is perhaps the original interactive installation art. The experience is challenging to the body so that the mind stops chattering with everyday distractions; it is four (or maybe even five) dimensional, engaging all of the senses and occupying space and time. The enormity of the experience leaves a resonance that lasts far into the future.

In order to pray, or request something from the deity of a shrine, it is necessary to make an offering. Most shrines have coin coffers for monetary donations—toss a coin, say a prayer, bow and ring the bell; sometimes clapping is also involved. Visitors may also purchase various types of materials on which to write prayers and then hang them as an offering. A third alternative offering is food—or because Shrine deities are known to be a jolly lot—sake or beer! At Fushimi Inari Shrine there is yet another alternative—torii gates. There are small gates available for purchase that are added to the hundreds of small sub-shrines. Then there are the large and *really* large votive torii that we passed under—these were donated by individual families or businesses. The cost? Somewhere between $15,000 and $300,000 each. And they don't last. Eventually the paint fades, the bottoms rot out and they have to be replaced. A message in practice about the transitory nature of life.

Torii Gates, 2009. Photograph: Lori Ellis.

Kyoto Streets
Wednesday, March 11, 2009

We call it "wending" when we take the less direct route or get a little lost on purpose. Kyoto is perhaps the most walkable city I have ever enjoyed as a pedestrian. After a month and a half of crisscrossing the entire city from large thoroughfares to tiny back streets, I have not found anywhere that it is not safe and enjoyable to walk in terms of traffic or personal safety. Neighborhoods have slightly different atmospheres, but the organization seems like what we referred to in New Orleans as a patchwork. A little bit of every kind of structure in every neighborhood.

Kyoto Streets, 2009. Photograph: Lori Ellis.

Getting around
Saturday, March 21, 2009

Though I am a diehard pedestrian, getting around a big city requires a combination of means. There are plenty of choices here, and all seem to be used equally . . . subway, bus, train, trolley, taxi, private auto, moped, motorcycle and bicycle. Devices that double as walkers and shopping baskets are used by the very elderly. Bicycles are ridden by citizens of all ages and include child seats and baskets for groceries etc. There are many bicycle parking lots. Interestingly, bicycles are almost never locked (I've only seen two that were) and items such as helmets and umbrellas are often left with the bicycle.

Buses are a bit more of a challenge, but with some familiarity of place names, the system unravels and becomes quite accessible. I just love the electronic bus kiosks—a three-stage marker indicates an approaching bus. Bus rides come with a chorus of sounds; the electronic announcement of stops is usually a very sweet female voice, the door closing warning [sounds like toby-da-shimadimas] repeats three times very, very fast; the high note is a bell tone indicating that a passenger wants to get off at the next stop; and it is all underscored by the characteristic intonation of the bus drivers, which is a cross between a bass and the last bit of air escaping from a bellows.

Kyoto station is the hub of most travel in and out of town. It is the largest and most modern building in the city. With tracks and terminals, it spans about two city blocks by four city blocks. Once I started thinking of it like an airport and just followed the signs, it stopped being intimidating. Like most modern airports, it houses a couple of malls, scores of restaurants and occasional art exhibitions . . . .

Train Station, **2009. Photograph: Lori Ellis.**

Turtle's Pace
Sunday, March 29, 2009

I've been giving a bit of thought to how and how fast people move through the city. Native Kyotoites have a relatively relaxed gait that takes them through daily travels whether walking downtown, in neighborhood streets, in the grocery store or to the bus stop. The pace picks up a bit in the subway at rush hour, but much less so than in New York. Contrary to that, it seems to be standard to walk/jog from place to place while involved in certain work activities.

An entirely different pace is practiced in restaurant service where movement is extraordinarily graceful and harmonious. During a tea ceremony or in a traditional restaurant there is yet another pace: tiny graceful steps, kneel on the tatami, put down items, slide open the shoji door, enter with tiny steps, kneel again, take items from outside to inside, close shoji, pick up items, walk with tiny steps, kneel on tatami, deliver items, etc.

Both national and international tourists seem to move according to their camera's pace: walk quick, stop, photo; walk quick, stop, photo; walk quick, wait for someone else to finish photo; walk quick to next photo. It would be interesting to make a map of a place based on where tourists stop for photos. Or to see if you could change established pathways by creating a photo-op. (I'm sure tourist boards all over the world are ahead of me on this one).

Historically, Kyoto's garden designers have used a number of strategies to control the movements of their viewers. Like the dry landscape gardens, there are living gardens meant to be seen from a single-seated position. The elements in these gardens are revealed by time. Like in two-dimensional art, the most contrasting elements are the first to be seen, the more subtle elements reward a patient observer. There are also layers of meaning for the well-educated viewer such as literary or spiritual references (I'm still trying to unravel these). There are also many types of stroll gardens where the viewer's attention is directed so that through time and movement, elements of the garden are hidden and then revealed. The walking pace is controlled by direction, pathway materials, and intentional pathway obstructions.

Turtle's Pace, **2009. Photograph: Lori Ellis.**

Construction
Saturday, April 11, 2009

There are wonderful little things about daily life in Kyoto that don't make the tourist guides or the art and art history texts. But then again, as an artist I find my attention being called to seemingly odd things at home as well. I spent a whole year while living in New Orleans, visiting home construction sites on off hours. I am fascinated by the process of construction in general, and am quite taken with the unique character of the construction projects here . . . .

Construction, 2009. Photograph: Lori Ellis.

Editor's note: For Lori Ellis's complete Kyoto blog, please go to:
http://www.loriellis.com/loriellis.com/Kyoto_blog/Kyoto_blog.html

Site-seeing

Meggan Gould

Bowdoin College

Abstract

In Site-seeing, I look to address the disciplinary structures surrounding photographic vision through a series of photographs in which I have removed the camera from its habitual proximity to the eye, allowing it greater corporeal liberty. Through this series of mobility-induced images, I seek to explore the visual experience of embodied interstitiality, of being at neither point A nor point B, but caught in motion between the two.

In *Site-seeing*, I look to address the disciplinary structures surrounding photographic vision through a series of photographs in which I have removed the camera from its habitual proximity to the eye, allowing it greater corporeal liberty. The images in this series are photographed while walking, driving, bicycling, gliding through landscapes on buses or trains. The continuity of my motion is not interrupted for the shutter's blink; the camera, clenched in my right hand, documents as much the swing of my step as it does the subject that triggered my finger to press the shutter release. Often, in fact, the latter escapes the frame altogether—hand/eye/subject/shutter coordination is surprisingly difficult at 60 miles per hour—and the processed film reveals fragments of the passing landscape that I often do not remember having seen.

Through this series of mobility-induced images, I seek to explore the visual experience of embodied interstitiality, of being at neither point A nor point B, but caught in motion between the two. The images are seen as 4 x 6 inch prints, evocative of the picture postcards that are sent or collected as evidence of a successful voyage to a specific site. Instead of postcards of the end point of a voyage, the Destination, I present postcards of the voyage itself, of the dynamism inherent to the journey, of the blur—and often beauty—of the mundane world traveled through on the way to the Scenic Overlook. These images reject the glossy, hygienic conventions in tourist photography, where the postcards available for purchase at the kiosk overlooking the Destination—be it canyon, monument, battlefield, or cityscape—cannot but be simulacral in nature; we stand for a few brief moments, witnessing the landscape stretched out before us, and allowing the color—saturated, static version prettily packaged in the postcard we will buy to send to our family to supercede our vision of the clouds, the rubbish bins, the fellow tourists jostling for the best view.

I present this series, which now constitutes hundreds of images, unedited. The formal pleasure of some of the images—the rhythm of a passing pedestrian stride, the stark isolation of an abandoned car in the middle of a field—must be seen in the context of the vast quantity of unremarkable images—too blurry, too skewed, perhaps—that are documents of the tedious, ill-focused monotony that constitutes much of daily motion. The temptation to highlight the more "successful" images is a false lure as Clément Chéroux points out in his *Fautographie—Petite histoire de l'erreur photographique,*

> The fickleness of [photographic] errors is essentially that they are the responsibility of those that judge them as such. The verdict relies on the person who pronounces it, and, thus, the context in which he/she is located—a context greatly determined by the here and now."[1] (Chéroux, 2003, p. 42)

The notion of photographic error must be reconsidered in an exercise such as this series; it is rather the hundreds of images as a whole—good, bad, or indifferent as they might be judged—that are used to probe a larger theoretical issue than the success of individual images. To carefully edit a series such as this, to glean all but the most formally pleasing images, would be to contradict its purpose. Movement through landscape, and our vision thereof, is not "picture-perfect;" it is indistinct half-glances, missed chances as we round corners, moments of clarity foregrounded with motion blur. Graham MacPhee aptly states: "Vision has come to imply a paradigm of meaningfulness based on clarity and coherence, against which alternative forms of experience are cast as aberrant, incoherent, and false" (MacPhee, 2002, p. 17). The decision to not edit this series allows me to insist that these latter, "alternative" visual experiences are not cast as aberrant. To favor some of the resulting images over others would be to reify the popular conception of clarity and formality that I question in the experience of vision.

These images, or instances of landscape, were recorded in France, South Africa, Zanzibar, Zambia, New York, Florida, Germany; they attempt to document the experience of active reception, nose pressed against the glass, watching the countryside or city streets pass by. How we interact with spaces unrolling on either side of us—both as we speed through them in our daily journeys and when we assign ourselves the role of 'tourist' in new places, intrigues me, for the experiences are dissimilar. In this series I am away from home, traveling as a passenger in unknown territory, concentrating on my role as viewer, attempting to photograph the gaze of the embodied viewer. As it is this gaze itself that interests me, I do not separate the resulting photographs by place—continent, city, or state—or by physical means of transportation—foot, automobile, or train, the distinction is only a matter of relative speed; the experience of my traveler's gaze remains constant.

I have chosen to present these images, unedited and irrespective of physical location upon firing of the shutter, following the form of an extensive grid, covering the entire space of a wall. As Rob Shields indicates, albeit in the context of mapping cyberspace:

> Grids are a modernist model of space . . . . The grid of the nineteenth-century colonial map imposed latitude and longitude to encompass, define and therefore possess all possible places. By having a potential grid reference of anywhere everywhere was reduced. On a grid, here and there are irrelevant (Shields, 2000, p. 149).

To impose a rigid structure on such disparate and undisciplined imagery is to reassert an element of control, via presentation, into the chaotic reality of the encounter with the embodied viewer. In so doing I can confirm the irrelevancy of place as well as disallow the dominance of any individual image, allowing the viewer the freedom to meander through the photographs much as I did through the landscapes—doubling back, taking a side road, or carrying on straight through the frenzied mix of motion blur and haphazard focus of which my own myriad voyages were constituted.

Notes

[1] "L'inconstance des erreurs repose essentiellement sur celui qui les juge comme telles . . . Le verdict dépend donc de celui qui l'énonce et, par conséquent, de l'environnement culturel où il se situe. Ce contexte étant très largement déterminé par son ici et maintenant."

References

Chéroux, C. (2003). *Fautographie-petite histoire de l'erreur photographique.* Crisnée, Belgium: Yellow Now.

MacPhee, G. (2002). *The architecture of the visible.* London: Continuum.

Shields, R. (2000). Hypertext links: The ethic of the index and its space-time effects. In A. Herman and T. Swiss (Eds.), *The World Wide Web and contemporary cultural theory* (pp. 145-160). New York: Routledge.

Editor's note: To see a grid of Meggan Gould's photographs, please go to: http://appweb.cortland.edu/ojs/index.php/Wagadu/article/view/419/736

Stroller Flâneur

Katerie Gladdys

University of Florida

Abstract

Pushing a baby stroller, I examine the minutiae of my suburban neighborhood, searching for patterns and narratives in the genealogies of architectural structures and topographies while simultaneously searching for items of interest for my son. My resulting observations collage both real and imagined systems into metaphors of community. The methodology informing this video is a gendered riff on the practice of the flâneur where the necessity of childcare becomes a platform for textualizing suburban space.

I push my son in a stroller through the neighborhood. Wandering with no agenda other than outside time with my child, I reflect upon this locomotion that constitutes the most public and stereotyped activities of motherhood. The pace of the walk forces me to notice the minutiae of suburbia, examining the environment for patterns and narratives. Semi-tropical Florida, Home-Depot domesticity, traces of the historic—but little known—Liberty Hill African-American community, evidence of the current recession, and the omnipresent desperate drone of condominium construction collide in the geography that constitutes my local. I attempt to discern the genealogy of architectural structures and topographies, visually leafing through the layers of additions, subtractions, road surfaces and plantings. Simultaneously, I search for items of possible interest to my son—animals, vehicles, and lawn decorations. With the advent of intelligible speech, he, too, participates in this free association. A dialectic emerges between me, my son, and my surroundings that recalls my own history. I wonder if the presence of my son intensifies that which evokes nostalgia for the past/ my childhood.

My observations of the local environment become a collage of both real and imagined systems that serve as metaphors for understanding the place where I live. The data of these habitual walks is the accretion of perusals followed by a distillation of "whatever is worth emphasizing as a specimen of significant transformations of the public scene" (Morowski, 1994, p. 188). Time is spent gleaning resources associated with homemaking—fallen fruit, cast-off furniture, baby gear and toys—and locating the exotic in the personalized details of mass-produced architecture and topographies— recollecting England in the second-floor windows of a faux Tudor cottage, ascertaining the origin of the plants in people's yards—Lowe's ready-mades or specimens from a local nursery, peering into the lit windows and open garages, manufacturing narratives determined by a limited glimpse of an interior, writing biographies based upon the bumper stickers affixed to parked vehicles, deciphering the layers of pavement and road surfaces for clues that belie a history older than I.

The methodology that informs this piece is a gendered riff on the practice of the flâneur where the necessity of childcare is the platform for textualizing suburban space. My version of flânerie is a spatial practice (à la de Certeau) of my neighborhood and the surrounding environs. The performance of strolling a child is indeed one of the social processes of inhabiting and appropriating the public spaces of the suburbs as well as of the city. The path that I take through this space of my neighborhood is variable, the route determined by season, weather, time, and mood, stops occurring for snacks, the occasional diaper change.

> What better way to reassure oneself, to remap the local, than to tour its transformed streets? . . . The gaze of the flâneur is thus part of a tactic to appropriate not only the local, physical spaces of the city as one's own 'turf' . . . but also to participate in the popular sense of empire and to master and even revel in the 'emporium' [Substitute suburbia for emporium] (Shields, 1994, p. 74).

The physical manifestation of the piece, *Stroller Flâneur*, is a video of pushing my son in a stroller around the neighborhood. Taking structural cues from Benjamin's *Arcades Project*, I document my experience of walking, looking and researching this place by collecting the multi-faceted, often conflicting, signifiers of familiar suburbia to create a fractured, even strange, landscape. Several layers of audio and video are composited, forming strata of imagery—my child in the stroller, the neighborhood, virtual Google representations of the neighborhood, aerial photography, property tax assessment maps, my voice, ambient noise. My visual and aural observations periodically interrupt and focus the viewers' attention on particular aspects of the landscape with the intention to create polymorphic narratives. Flânerie is a call to participate, to play. It does not strive for accuracy, but asks those who do read its products according to Hessel to "go yourself just like me without destination on the small journeys of discovery of the fortuitous" (as cited in Frisby, 1994, p. 96). I endeavor to awaken the curiosity for the quotidian in my viewers: transforming spectators into participants yearning to explore their surrounding environments.

References

Benjamin, W. (2002). *The arcades project*. Cambridge: Belknap Press of Harvard University Press.

De Certeau, M. (2002). *The practice of everyday life*. Berkeley: University of California Press.

Frisby, D. (1994). The flâneur in social theory. In K. Tester (Ed.), *The flâneur* (pp. 81-110). London, England: Routledge.

Morawski, S. (1994). The hopeless game of flânerie. In K. Tester (Ed.), *The flâneur* (pp. 181-197). London, England: Routledge.

Shields, R. (1994). Fancy footwork: Walter Benjamin's notes on flânerie. In K. Tester (Ed.), *The flâneur* (pp. 81-110). London, England: Routledge.

Editor's note: To see Katerie Gladdys's complete video, go to: http://appweb.cortland.edu/ojs/index.php/Wagadu/article/view/406/737

she's walking . . .

Henry Gwiazda

Minnesota State University Moorhead

Abstract

In she's walking . . . a virtual woman takes a walk in a suburban neighborhood. She observes many types of movement—a car passes, the light changes, a volleyball is kicked, a nearby highway resounds. The interactions of movement fascinate her, and she discovers a kinetic narrative lying just underneath the banal surface of her surroundings. The scenes she observes, and unwittingly becomes a part of, link together in a larger artistic event.

A woman, in her early thirties, is walking on the sidewalk of a suburban neighborhood. The houses are identical architecturally with slight differences only in color. She is wearing white cotton pants and a light green sweater with a twill texture. Her brown hair is up.

She walks for four seconds in a straight line, stops, folds her arms and looks to her left,

> (indistinct sound of distant traffic from a highway)
> lowers her left arm almost 90 degrees and turns her neck also to the left.

She is looking at a house across the street. It has two levels with a porch in front. As she looks, the sunshine on the roof gradually increases. A gold Audi comes down the street in the lane closest to the house and the sunshine diminishes.

(traffic sounds end)

The car passes by.

The woman slowly stretches both her arms out and turns to her right about 35 degrees. There is an embankment about five feet high that rises suddenly from the sidewalk. On this embankment, some 15 feet from her is another house, identical to the one across the street. Because of the sun's angle, the side of the house facing her and the porch are in shadow. Through a large glass window she can see inside the house. The only sign of life is a dog on the porch. It's a grayish color with its front half in shadow and its rear half in light. It is motionless. She can also see part of the back porch of the next house up the street.

(Propeller airplane in the distance, the sound gradually getting louder for about 5 seconds)

A soccer ball arches gracefully in the air in the backyard.

(sound of traffic passing on an adjacent highway added to the airplane sound)

She turns and continues walking; the light on the sidewalk in front of her gets brighter. She stops, places her hands on her stomach and leans forward as if to look at something on the ground.

To her left, a cloud's shadow is moving very slowly, making the street darker and darker. As it reaches the roofs of the houses, a black man on a bicycle passes slowly from left to right going up the street. He is wearing maroon shorts and a white, short sleeve sweatshirt.

(sound of several birds)

The woman is now standing in a driveway that inclines 45 degrees up to a covered carport. She is looking at a bush on the right side of the driveway. Suddenly, she continues walking up the driveway toward the house. She stops in front of a large window divided into four panes and kneels on one knee, looking into the house.

In the house a man is standing, practicing electric guitar. He is bald, in his early thirties, wearing brown trousers and a white shirt buttoned up to the neck. The guitar is a reddish brown color. The interior of the house is sparse and modernist.

As he lifts his right hand almost imperceptibly to strike the strings, the woman lowers her head as if looking at the carpet in the house.

The guitarist moves his left wrist and finger almost at the top of the fret board, obviously using vibrato on a note we do not hear because of the closed windows. At the same time, two things occur.

(the sound of an airplane passing from left to right)

(a light shines on the guitarist's white shirt moving from right to left, then back to the right, changing shape, getting smaller until it comes to rest on the guitarist's chest)

He raises his head to look at the woman—

After a short pause, the woman stands up slowly, turns right and continues down the space between the house and a carport. Leaning against one of the carport's posts is a bicycle. She arrives in the backyard, which contains a shallow wading pool, a small outdoor covered sitting area, and a dog. The dog is sitting, facing the house and looking to its right. The woman sits down on the cement walkway. From the backyard, she can see a raised road or highway about a half mile away. Between the backyard and the raised highway is a smaller hill with sparse trees.

As the woman looks to her left the dog twists its head slightly.

(the sound of a bee)

A car appears on the berm going from left to right, the woman and dog turn to face each other, the dog looks down, and the woman raises her hand to the dog. At the same time the overall light on the ground gets brighter, causing a subtle shadow from one of the posts of the sitting area to appear on the grass.

(the bee stops)

Another car travels from right to left while the dog twists its head as if confused. The woman lowers her hand, looks to her left again and the sky darkens slightly, making the shadow disappear.

A third car travels from left to right, the light brightens quickly, the dog moves its front right leg up and to the left slightly, and looks up at the woman.

(the sounds of several bees)

The woman turns her head back to the dog, raises her hand, the light darkens, the dog looks to its right again while keeping its right front leg raised.

(the sound of the bees stops)

The woman looks up to her right at the sky while keeping her hand raised at the dog.

Editor's note: To see Henry Gwiazda's complete video, please go to:
http://appweb.cortland.edu/ojs/index.php/Wagadu/article/view/422/739